DO YOU WANT

INWARD POWER?

DO YOU WANT INWARD POWER?

BY

JOHN HEUSS

FOREWORD BY

HORACE W. B. DONEGAN

GREENWICH · CONNECTICUT

Printed in the United States of America

Designed by Stefan Salter

To Betty, my wife, who has shared our ministry for eighteen years, and who has helped me learn the meaning of gratitude to God.

FOREWORD

THESE sermons are the answers to religious questions that perplex and puzzle the mind of modern man. The rector of the most famous parish in America is aware that with exceptions, of course, the man in the pew has only vague and indefinite ideas about religion. It is likely that modern man has next to no knowledge of God, or who Jesus Christ is; or what Christianity teaches about man's duty and destiny. Nor has he any understanding of prayer, or grace, or salvation; or his need of them. Furthermore, he has inadequate ideas about the value of the Sacraments, and no true conception of the mission of the Church or whence it derives its authority. Yet these are the things that must be known about religion; they matter most of all.

The reader of this volume will be lead—as was the listener—to an understanding of the essentials of the Faith. He will be stimulated to further knowledge and study.

Dr. Heuss has unusual gifts of popular exposition of Christian doctrine. Here the Faith is presented in language modern man can understand. Like all true preachers he believes what he preaches, without any reservation or secret evasion of mind whatever. The man in the pulpit may be eloquent; his sermons may have literary excellence but unless he believes utterly the message he proclaims, his words will be but words.

I enthusiastically commend this book by one who not only makes careful preparation but also prays over his sermons as Milton prayed about his poems:

> Instruct me . . . .
> That to the height of this great argument
> I may assert Eternal Providence,
> and justify the ways of God to men.

HORACE W. B. DONEGAN

CONTENTS

WHAT ABOUT

REVELATION?

WHAT ABOUT REVELATION?

How that by revelation he made known . . . the mystery.—EPH. 3:3

ALL that is most surely believed among us has come first by the action of God. We believe that God took the initiative in making Himself known to men. God has revealed Himself to us. Therefore, the first great doctrine of the Christian religion is the belief that God has made a Revelation of what He is and what He expects of us.

The whole Christian religion begins with Revelation. Its truth has come to us by Revelation. In the final analysis, we are putting our trust in a Revelation.

Have you ever stopped to reflect on how few are the ways by which we come to know the truth about life? There are only four ways available to us.

One way is by means of guesswork. I suppose that that is what a good many people use most of the time. They make as good a guess as they can, and try not to worry too much about whether their guessing makes sense. The old familiar saying that "the moon is made of green cheese" is a good example of "guessing the answers to the riddle of nature." When our ancestors stoutly maintained that the earth was flat, they were guessing that this was so because, as far as they could see, it had all the appearances of being flat. There is a place for guesswork in life and, once in a while, all of us have to rely upon it. But, at its best, guessing rests upon speculation and is a very unsatisfactory way of knowing what life is all about.

Another way to know things is to reason them out. This is the method of logical thinking. You sit down and try to think out, within your mind, the answer to a riddle that bothers you. Suppose, for example, you were wondering how the Congregational Church in America began, you might reason as follows: The Pilgrim Fathers came to America in 1620; the Pilgrim Fathers were Congregationalists; therefore, all modern Congregationalists stem from the Pilgrim Fathers.

Logic, however, has its limitations, and, unless you are careful, it can get you into trouble. So much of its result depends on the premise from which you start to reason. For example, look what might happen to your thinking if you said: "All Pilgrim Fathers were Englishmen. The first Congregationalists were Pilgrim Fathers; therefore all Congregationalists today must be Englishmen!"

Another trouble with logic is that it deduces the particular from the general and does not care a fig about looking at the facts. So, when a man tells me that he believes in God or does not believe in God because he has thought it all out logically, I get worried; for logic cannot prove or disprove God. It all depends on the premise.

You can know a lot nowadays by means of research. Scientific investigation is the third way to know things. This certainly has been a most profitable way to useful knowledge for our day and age. Primitive mankind spent centuries guessing about the universe. Classical man in Greece and Rome reasoned about the riddle of existence. Modern man peers into a telescope or a microscope and says, "I am going to have a look at the facts. I will weigh this item, and I'll measure that item; I will compute how fast this other item is going; and I'll do it over and over again until I arrive at a general law which will describe how it works. This law I can then use again and again to get a desired result." Out of this experimental searching have come automobiles, aeroplanes, oil burners, iceboxes, and atom bombs!

Science indeed explains a great deal. But it does not explain everything. You cannot weigh out a half-ton of human love, for one thing. You cannot measure off six yards of courage and dole it out to a G.I. going into battle. It does not explain ambition, nor fear, nor grief, nor honor, nor guilt, nor loyalty, nor any of the inner spiritual capacities of Man. It can tell you that a man is physically composed of ninety-seven cents' worth of potassium, sodium, chlorine, hydrogen, nitrogen, and a dozen other simple chemicals. It can describe the average height, weight, and life-span of a man. But, when you are finished, does it describe any real man you know? Does it account for Shakespeare, Beethoven, Joe DiMaggio, or Lana Turner? And how do you account scientifically for Amos, who endangered his life to speak out against injustice among his fellow Jews? And, most of all, how do you account for Jesus Christ, and what He did and said as He died upon a cross?

I defy any scientist to show me just how he would reduce Verdi's capacity to write beautiful music to a scientific formula. Show me, if you can, the equation that will explain Raphael painting the Sistine Madonna. Then give me the infallible law that describes how Jesus happened to think up The Beatitudes!

You are amused! Of course, you are! No one can know these things scientifically any more than he can know them by logical reasoning. Most of the big, important things of human life cannot be known by scientific research.

There is a fourth way left for us to know things. This is the way of Revelation. We can know some of the most essential things about our existence because God has shown them to us. They have come to us by *His* action, not by ours. Indeed, it would seem that the most important of all of our knowledge came whether mankind liked the idea or not. We have often been the receivers of God's Revelation of Himself, not because of, but in spite of, ourselves. Take, as an example, our knowledge of the moral law. Man did not take kindly to the demands of the Ten Commandments when he first heard about them, and there is ample evidence that he does not go into ecstasies of delight over keeping them today.

Or, take the fact that Jesus Christ rose from the dead. Nobody expected *that* to happen! It was quite contrary to human logic. The Jews were confident that they had taken care of a very troublesome fellow. But "Him whom the Jews had slain, God raised up on the third day," and the troublesome Galilean was back. This time He was really troublesome; He split Judaism in twain. The Jews did not ask for the Risen

Christ. He was thrust upon them by the action of Almighty God.

Both the giving of the Ten Commandments and the Resurrection of the Lord Christ were Revelation —the action of God in making His purpose known.

If there is, then, this valid way for us to know about the meaning of life, we should ask ourselves how this Revelation has taken place.

Let us be absolutely certain about one thing: God's Revelation of Himself is not to be confused with the idea that every man has an inner voice of conscience in him which tells him what is right or wrong. No one will deny that such an inner voice exists. But Revelation was not given to every Tom, Dick, and Harry in the world as a general illumination of the heart and mind.

And, just as it was not a divine spark placed in the breast of every man, neither was Revelation given to us through a few highly placed official leaders such as kings, high priests, or men of acknowledged wisdom. God rarely took as His messengers those who held high positions of leadership. Indeed, His Revelation came to us from most unexpected sources. Abraham, an unknown desert wanderer, was called and became the Father of the Hebrew nation. An obscure nobody named Amos was called as he guarded his sheep in the lonely hill country of Tekoa.

He spoke words of fire about social justice that have burned down the corridors of the ages. A peasant girl named Mary was chosen and gave birth to the Son of God.

Revelation took place in certain great events in the lives of a few obscure people. These events turned out to have so much influence on the lives of other people that they changed the history of mankind.

Now can you not see clearly what Revelation is?

Revelation is not a theory about life. It is not a message or series of messages from inspired but fallible men. It is not a collection of theological propositions which have been put together by great scholars. Revelation is a series of decisive actions in history, preeminently that particular section of history covered by the Bible, by which God made Himself known in an unmistakable way. The clue to the meaning of Revelation is the word "action." God has intervened in history to "do" certain things. By looking at the record of what He has done, a record which modern historical research has served only to strengthen and make more clear, the Christian religion has learned what it believes. The Christian religion does not rest its case upon philosophical discussions about the nature of God. It does not rest its case upon any theological system of belief. It does not try to devise cunning intellectual explanations of the universe. It rests its case on the most substantial evidence obtainable. It takes its stand on certain verifiable historical events.

The Church has called these events the "Acts of God's Redemption of Mankind." These acts are all described in the Bible. They begin with the historical fact of the beginning of the Hebrew nation; reach their most dramatic point in the birth, life, suffering, death, resurrection, and ascension of Jesus Christ; they continue into history with the coming of the Holy Ghost to found a new order of changed men on earth in the fellowship of the Church; and will end when you and I and all other men stand at last before the Judgment Seat of God.

So far we have seen that some of life's most valuable understandings cannot come to us in any way except by Revelation. Then we recognized that, by Revelation, the Christian religion means the series of great historical, world-changing events recorded in the Bible. Now, let us conclude by giving a simple summary of those events:

The place to look for the most simple summary is in the creeds of the Church, which we say at the worship services. Some people have a badly mistaken idea about our Apostles' and Nicene Creeds. They make the mistake of thinking that they are a series of theological propositions. They are not even a short summary of systematic theology. They are a summary of Revelation. They are an ancient historical account of what God did, as recorded in the Bible. They describe the action of Redemption. Nearly every important word in the Creed is a verb.

Listen carefully and you will learn quickly what the content of God's Revelation is:

I BELIEVE IN GOD,

Who 1. *created* the heaven and earth,
Who 2. *sent* His only begotten Son Jesus Christ,
Who 3. for us men and for our salvation *came* down from heaven,
Who 4. was *incarnate* by the Holy Ghost of the Virgin Mary,
Who 5. *was made* Man,
Who 6. *was crucified* also for us under Pontius Pilate,
Who 7. *suffered* and *was buried,*
Who 8. on the third day *rose* again according to the Scriptures,
Who 9. *ascended* into heaven,
Who 10. *sitteth* on the right hand of the Father,
Who 11. *shall come* again, with glory, to *judge* both the quick and the dead.

I BELIEVE IN THE HOLY GHOST,

Who 12. *proceedeth* from the Father and the Son,

Who 13. is *worshipped* and *glorified,*
Who 14. *spake* by the prophets.

And then the summary ends with an account of that action of God, in which we are sharing now—the present life of the one Catholic and Apostolic Church —and an account of God's expected action, yet to come, when all the dead shall rise and the redeemed shall share eternally in the Life of the world to come.

> I believe one Catholic and Apostolic Church: I acknowledge one Baptism for the remission of sins: And I look for the Resurrection of the dead: And the life of the world to come.

If this is what we mean by Revelation, what then is the Christian man or woman's life of faith? What are you to do about the Revelation that God has given us of Himself? How does it affect your life?

If you are living in this Faith, then you are daily growing in a knowledge of this activity of God and are called to understand and take an active part in it yourself.

God has let loose into the world a powerful, relentless spiritual force, which is at work counteracting, forestalling, judging, defeating, overcoming, and redeeming all of the wickedness of evil man.

No matter what other responsibility life has placed upon you—whether of family, business, or profession —it is your first obligation as Christian men and women to pray and to work daily for the victory of God's revealed purpose for mankind.

WHAT ABOUT CREATION?

WHAT ABOUT CREATION?

Lift up your eyes on high, and behold who hath created these things. — ISA. 40:26a

AS LONG as man has been upon the earth, he has speculated upon the riddle of the universe. How did it begin? Was it always here? What caused it to exist? Is there any purpose to it? Will it ever end?

The Psalmist looked out upon creation and sang: "The heavens declare the glory of God; and the firmament showeth His handy-work."

Few thinking men have been contented to conclude that the universe is meaningless.

While it will always remain filled with mystery, because the tiny mind of man is not great enough to understand all of its secrets, most men see enough to convince them that

The spacious firmament on high,
With all the blue ethereal sky,
And spangled heavens, a shining frame,
Their great Original proclaim.

The unwearied sun, from day to day,
Does his Creator's power display,
And publishes to every land,
The work of an Almighty hand.

What though in solemn silence all
Move round the dark terrestial ball;
What though no real voice or sound
Amidst their radiant orbs are found;
In Reason's ear they all rejoice,
And utter forth a glorious voice,
Forever singing as they shine,
"The hand that made us is divine."*

When we try to understand our own life and the world we live in, there are only three choices that we can make to explain creation.

We can conclude that our existence is a *meaningless accident.*

> "We men and women may be the casual offspring of an unmeaning process which has spawned us on the surface of this planet, and will again engulf us when our brief span of life is over. Meanwhile, we may as well make the best of a bad job, and get through our lives with as little discomfort and as much satisfaction as possible."†

*Hymn 309, *The Hymnal,* 1940. Words by Joseph Addison based on Psalm XIX.

† *Christian Faith and Practice* by Leonard Hodgson, pp. 18-19 (New York: Scribner). Used by permission.

We should recognize that a great many people nowadays believe that this is true. They see the universe as a place where chance has brought together a variety of chemical combinations. Some combinations are lifeless like the planets in the sky. Others for a time, like plants and animals and men, possess the quality of life. But live matter soon becomes dead matter. Chemicals are constantly changing combinations. This has always taken place and will go on forever. All creation is the result of a blind, purposeless, mechanical hitching and unhitching of the atomic elements of which all things are composed.

In such a world view there is no place for God. He is not needed because the atoms do it all themselves.

In such a world view there can be no purpose because there is no way of telling what the atoms will be doing next.

With such a world view what is the common sense way for a man to live? To try to avoid getting hurt. To try to be as comfortable as possible.

Oddly enough, this explanation of creation has produced in modern times two exactly opposite philosophies of life and two exactly opposite kinds of people. On the one hand, it has led to a blatant form of amoral, individualistic materialism. On the other hand, it has led to the vicious curse of Russian Communism.

Both grew out of a skeptical explanation of the universe. The one tries to solve the problem of life by letting each individual cushion himself against the possibility of pain as best he can by his own efforts. The other is even more skeptical and believes that an all-powerful state must ruthlessly obtain security for all.

Both of these philosophies originated in a pseudo-scientific, modern, mechanical interpretation of creation—an interpretation in which there was no room for final purpose. It is no wonder that in every nation, where blatant individualism has run riot for awhile, it is not long before a demonic statism challenges it.

If this understanding of creation prevails, it can destroy the modern world. It acknowledges no restraining moral power, and it is free to use force in any shape or form to achieve its desired end.

This is why the question, "Are you a religious man?" is today the most important question in the world. The first religious question to ask a man is not, "What do you think about belonging to a church?" but "What is your interpretation of the universe?" Whether or not he does anything about the church will depend on how he explains the mystery of creation.

Fortunately, there are other ways to explain creation than that of the atheistic, skeptical materialist's.

I shall go for a moment to the opposite extreme.

The second way we have to explain the universe recognizes that it was *created by God* and that, if we only understood all about it, we would see that,

All are parts of one stupendous whole,
Whose body nature is, and God the soul;
That changed through all, and yet in all the same,
Great in the earth, as in th'ethereal frame,
As full, as perfect in vile man that mourns,
As the rapt seraphim, that adores and burns;
All nature is but art, unknown to thee;
All chance, direction, which thou cans't not see;
All discord, harmony not understood;
All partial evil, universal good.*

Human thought, in its effort to solve the problem of the meaning of life, swings like a pendulum between two extreme ideas. Either it sweeps away all notion that God has any place left in a mechanical creation or it jumps to the opposite conclusion that the universe is so filled in every part by God that even the bad things, which seem to happen in it, are actually universal good. This explanation is called pantheism.

The men who hold to the first idea become grossly materialistic. Those who accept the second are guilty of using religion as an escape mechanism.

* Excerpts from *The Essay on Man* by Alexander Pope.

Let me be certain that you do not misunderstand what I am saying. This second explanation of the universe, which so completely spiritualizes all of nature that the actual world of our everyday experiences begins to dissolve away, is not to be confused with the Holy Catholic Church's faith in the goodness and ultimate triumph of God.

What this extreme spiritual interpretation of creation tries to do is to make you and me believe that there is no reality whatever to the physical world in which we live or to the physical bodies our souls inhabit.

Those who hold this opinion have to live as though both matter and pain do not exist.

This is by no means a new idea. I cannot say whether or not Mary Baker Eddy had ever read any of the ancient philosophers of Greece and Rome. I am inclined to believe that she had not, but the truth is that she was not the first to believe that matter is only appearance and that only mind is real.

At the time when the early Christian Church was struggling to think out the full meaning of its Faith, there were a variety of Graeco-Roman mystery cults that held to a philosophy known as Gnosticism. This word comes from the Greek word *gnosis* that means "to know." The Gnostics claimed to have a special knowledge about the universe. The main idea in this knowledge was that the physical world was a complete illusion. To them matter did not exist. Only the spiritual had reality.

By the sixth century A.D., this strange idea had pretty well died out. It was not revived until the seventeenth century, when it began to find a milder expression in the poetic writings of men like Alexander Pope and William Shakespeare. In *The Tempest* (Act IV, Sc. 1) Shakespeare wrote:

> . . . . . We are such stuff
> As dreams are made on, and our little life
> Is rounded with a sleep.

Now in the twentieth century it is back in our midst again in its most extreme expression as the religion of the Christian Scientist.

If you accept this explanation of creation, you believe that you are a creature of pure spiritual nature, trapped in what appears to be a lower material environment. You will be religious, and you will believe firmly in God as the materialist does not. But you will believe that the main purpose of your life will be to escape from the carnal prison you are in.

If you do it by persuading yourself that matter and pain are an illusion, you will be near to Christian Science. If you do it by trying to stamp out the world and the flesh from all share in human life, you will become a modern Puritan.

In neither case will you be believing or practicing the doctrine of creation as it is understood by the Holy Catholic Church.

There is a third way to explain the universe and the life of Man.

You can believe that creation is the work of God, all of it made by Him, both in its visible and invisible parts. Nor did He merely get it started somehow out of nothing, and then leave it to run itself. He has been working in creation constantly to accomplish an unswerving, intelligible purpose.

This purpose has been to bring into existence other beings who, at least in some ways, are like Him. God wanted something in the universe that could love Him and voluntarily cooperate with His almighty will. We men are this creation that bears His image. We alone can think and will and love as He does.

In order to give us these capacities, God had to allow us a margin of free will. If we are to be free enough to love at all, God has to take the chance that we will misuse our freedom.

Thus, the gift of freedom means either that we can love or not love, do good or do harm, create beauty or destroy it.

Out of man's misuse of freedom springs the evil of the world.

Now notice something very important. Right here is where the genuine Christian differs sharply from the materialist on one hand and from the pantheist on the other.

The materialist says that evil consists in physical inconvenience and physical pain. He solves the problem of evil either by providing as much individual luxury as he can for himself or, if he is a Communist, by trying to create a classless society.

The pantheist says that evil is an illusion. He tries to meet it by persuading himself that it does not exist.

> All chance direction, which thou cans't not see:
> All discord, harmony not understood;
> All partial evil, universal good.

But the Christian says that evil and matter are both realities that have to be wrestled with in deeds and cannot be cured by thought alone.

How does the Christian solve the problem of evil? He knows that by his own unaided effort he cannot solve it. He believes that God has acted in history to overcome the evil that is caused by man's misuse of freedom.

He believes that God entered human life in Jesus Christ and wrestled with evil in the flesh.

He believes that, when Christ died upon the cross, God was in fact doing battle with the ultimate in evil.

This means that whenever you have to undergo pain, you have the full assurance that God stands close in utmost sympathy with what you have to bear. He knows what pain is like because He has been through the worst of it in flesh akin to yours.

The reason why the cross has always been the most precious symbol of our faith is that whenever we look upon it, whenever we make the sign of the cross upon ourselves, we are strengthened by the powerful recollection of the way Jesus handled life's central problem as He suffered and died.

Christ did not go down into defeat before pain. He did not deny that it existed. No, He took all that pain had to give, and He sanctified it, making that which was in itself horrible into that which was so beautiful that mankind has never been able to forget Him upon His cross. That is why the stark cross of Good Friday is wrapped around with the lilies of Easter Day.

But it means an even greater victory over evil than the moral victory Christ won as He died upon the cross.

On Easter Day, Jesus Christ was alive again. Even death, the final realistic fact of mankind's vulnerability, is swallowed up in victory.

It is no wonder that Saint Paul wrote in jubilation to the Corinthian Church: "O death, where is thy sting? O grave, where is thy victory?"

We Christians believe that God is the creator of all things. We believe that man's evil has spoiled a part of God's creation. But we believe that God through His mighty action overcame evil.

> But thanks be to God, which giveth us the victory through our Lord Jesus Christ.

WHAT DOES GOD

DO ABOUT EVIL?

WHAT DOES GOD DO ABOUT EVIL?

. . . who can forgive sins but God only?
—Mark 2:7

WE ARE thinking about the six great doctrines of the Christian Faith. We have seen that our belief is founded on the solid rock of God's actions in history. God has revealed Himself unmistakably by His deeds. Therefore, the first great doctrine of our Faith is the Doctrine of Revelation.

We have considered how a Christian understands the universe about him. His understanding is the doctrine of creation. Only three explanations are possible. You can be a materialist; you can be a pantheist; you can be a genuine Christian.

We reject materialism because, denying the existence of God, it is cynical and cruel. We reject pantheism because, denying the evil of mankind, it is sentimental and silly. We conclude that, in the universe, God and evil are both real. This is why some people find it hard to accept Christianity. If God is good, why does He permit evil?

The doctrine of creation leaves us with the question, What does God do about evil? Let us think about this now. I do not mind giving you a little clue to the answer. We are talking about the Doctrine of the Atonement.

The materialist and the Christian have only one thing in common. Both take the reality of evil seriously. I think I can make crystal-clear how they differ in their understanding of what evil is, because each one interprets evil differently and each has a different solution to it.

The materialist believes that there are *three* kinds of evil. The Christian goes him one better and insists that there are four. As a matter of fact, the Christian claims that if you do not recognize the fourth kind of evil, and do something about it, it is absolute folly to waste your time thinking you can do away with the other three. I believe you will see how right the Christian is.

What are the first three forms of evil that both the materialist and Christian agree exist?

The *first* is the evil of *ignorance.* Surely this is a most repugnant evil. Ask anyone who has ever been to India, where ignorance is rife, what it is like. Sickness, brutality, and superstition flourish. So dreadful an evil is it that, in our generation, every nation in the world is trying its best to stamp it out.

The *second form* is the evil of *human suffering.* Pain in a thousand ways plagues mankind. We are born in pain. Either it haunts us as a possiblity or it strikes us down as a ghastly reality, every hour of our life. Suffering is caused by disease. Suffering is caused by war. Suffering is caused by poverty. Suffering is caused by what people do to other people. Mankind is unbelievably inhuman toward his own species.

The *third form* is the evil of *ugliness.* God made nature beautiful. Man has a singular gift for defacing nature's loveliness. The landscape of America is littered with hideous billboards. Every city spawns its ugly slums. Souvenir hunters destroy everything unguarded. People write their names in public places. Lunch boxes litter every picnic site. Left to his own devices, man would rather wallow in filth than bother to be orderly.

These three evils—ignorance, suffering, ugliness—are the universally recognized Trinity of Hell. Whenever anyone decides to crusade against evil, it is usually one of these three forms that he is anxious to eliminate.

But there is a *fourth kind* of evil. This is called *sin.* The materialist does not recognize that it exists. Here is where the Christian differs sharply from him. So strong is this difference that the Christian claims "unless mankind overcomes sin, it is utterly impossible to deal effectively with any other form of evil!"

Let me illustrate how right the Christian is. A materialist might do valiant battle to eliminate ignorance by making education available to all. The Christian will say "God bless you, but do not forget that knowledge is not enough." An educated devil is able to do more harm than an ignorant peasant. Ignorance does not create a devil. Sin does!

If you are really going to do something about evil, do not stop with your efforts to eliminate ignorance, suffering, and ugliness. Underneath each one of these is a deeper problem. Underneath every other evil is the evil of sin!

Now what is the difference between these first three and sin? Ignorance, suffering, and ugliness are all evils that strike man from outside himself. *Sin is the corruption of man's internal nature.*

That is why sin is the most serious of the four. It is conceivable that by our own efforts we might be able to rid the world of the first three. It is absolutely impossible for man to cure himself of sin.

The reason why all reform efforts that leave out the reality of sin fail is that sin obstructs our efforts to deal with any other kind of evil.

How blind can mankind be! It was sin that destroyed the greatness that was Rome. Sin corrupted the medieval church. Sin is the slimy thing that is reducing the waterfront of New York City to a gang-ridden nightmare of brutality, graft, and murder. Sin lies behind the tragic incapacity of New York City to run an efficient government and to deal with crime.

It is not ignorance. It is not human suffering. It is not ugliness that is our real enemy. To deal with these alone is to scratch the surface of things. If the world is going to be any better, we must find a way to deal with *sin!*

It is at this point that some alert person will speak up and say, "All right. I see that sin is the hard core of all evil. But I want to know two things: Why, if God is good, does He permit evil to exist? And, if every well-intentioned effort Man makes to rid himself of evil fails, just what does God offer as a solution that is any better? How does He deal with sin?"

Allow me to tackle the first question first. When God created the universe, He created nothing that was not good. It is a logical impossibility to believe, if God is perfect goodness, that anything which He created could in itself be evil. To believe that God is not good is to destroy His right to be God at all. Therefore, God's creation is all good. No evil can come from Him.

We agreed, also, that evil is created by mankind. Why does God allow such a thing to happen? The only answer that makes sense is that it is God's intention to create people who are able to respond voluntarily to His will. To be able to do this, God has to give man freedom. Evil is the result of man's deliberate misuse of freedom. Whatever ignorance there is, whatever suffering there is, whatever ugliness there is, we have them because man, by his misuse of freedom, is internally corrupt. Evil is the dangerous potential by-product of man's capacity to love God and voluntarily to do His will. This is the reason we have evil in the world.

"Well," you ask, "why does God put up with it? Why doesn't God put an end to mass rebellion?" If He did, He would have to destroy our freedom. We would become automatons. His purpose in creating us forever would be thwarted. God cannot blot out evil by some great cosmic act of destruction. If He did, what He set out to accomplish in His universe never can come to pass. He set out at the beginning of creation to bring into existence creatures who voluntarily will choose to love Him and do His righteous will. It is conceivable that He may become so fed up with our selfish rebellion that He will, in disgust, destroy us. But the evidence indicates that this is not His solution to the evil of mankind. God permits evil to exist, though He does not condone it, because He is working out a purpose in which men, with dangerous freedom, play the central part.

Now we are ready for the crux of the questions we

are trying to understand. We know what evil really is. It is the corruption of our internal selves. This is known as *sin.* We also grasp why a God of goodness continues to allow evil to exist.

Let us come to grips with the second question asked. "If God is not condoning evil, what is He doing about it?"

We can arrive at a very clear answer if we consider for a moment a daily experience in the life of each one of us.

Suppose I were to do an injury to any one of you. Think carefully about what effect it might have upon you. Two possible things can happen. On the one hand, it may stir up in your heart a deep feeling of anger and resentment. Because I am a clergyman, the disillusionment may be so great that you will lose faith in every clergyman. Indeed, you may become so bitter and revengeful that you not only will give up going to church, but you may burn to get back at me in full retaliation. If all of this happens to you—or if any part of it happens to you—what I did to hurt you will have made you a worse person than you were in the beginning!

Now suppose that I suddenly begin to feel sorry for the injury I have done. Suppose I say, "I wish I had not hurt you. I want to undo the evil of which I have been the cause." Can I, of my own wishing and doing, undo the injury I have caused? Of course, I cannot. It has passed out of my personal control. Only you can help me atone for it. Whether or not you will be willing to help me make it up depends upon what you have allowed my evil to do to you. If you are bitter and revengeful, I can be sorry, but I cannot be forgiven!

But notice what the opposite of this implies. If I find that you have taken the injury in such a way that you have steadfastly refused to let it have any bad effect upon you, miraculously, you have cut short the power of my evil to be a source of further harm. Not only will my injury not harm you, but your action will have prevented my sin from muddying the stream of human life!

If I come to you now and say, "I am sorry," I will immediately receive forgiveness. It is only by such absorbing love and forgiveness that anything can be done about evil.

Apply this understandable human experience to God Himself.

God cannot solve the problem of human evil merely by letting the universe run its course. He has to do something about evil in that particular part of His creation where it arises. This is the sphere of human history.

We already have seen how clear it is that God has

acted in history. He first did something about evil when He inspired the minds of ancient men to know the difference between right and wrong. He spoke to men by the prophets, but this was not enough. It is an indisputable historical fact that a man named Jesus Christ lived. In the life and death of this man Jesus, the Christian sees God Himself acting to solve the evil of the world.

Now remember our own experience. You and I have the power to cut evil short by the way we take injury.

As Christ was nailed to the Cross, His prayer was, "Father, forgive them." The more He was tortured, the more intensely He loved. The more He suffered, the more He loved. And He loved the most as He was dying.

Christ died with love unconquered. He died with no bitterness, no remorse, no feelings of revenge. Here was a perfection of love that nothing is able to surpass. Whenever anyone has believed that this was God, it has touched a responsive chord in the sinful heart. It is the sight of God pouring out His love upon the Cross that has made hardened sinners penitent. Because God has absorbed the worst evil of mankind, He is able to forgive us our sins.

This is what God has done about evil. He does not strike first at ignorance. He does not enter His world to put a stop to human suffering. He does not wipe out the ugliness which we have spawned upon the earth. These evils He knows that redeemed men can solve. But the only men who can solve these evils are men who first are sorry for their own sin. The only men who will ever make this world a better place to live in are men who first know what it means to be forgiven by Almighty God. Only such men are so forgetful of self that they are able to absorb and lessen the evil of the world. Only such men are able to cooperate with God's creative will.

This is the kind of man God wants each one of us to be.

WHAT ABOUT CHRIST?

WHAT ABOUT CHRIST?

. . . the right faith is that we believe and confess: that our Lord Jesus Christ . . . is God and Man.—THE ATHANASIAN CREED

WE HAVE been thinking about the six great doctrines of the Christian Faith.

Earlier in this series I tried to show you what God does about evil. We agreed that, if Jesus Christ were really God, His suffering and His death on the Cross demonstrated that God effectively deals with evil.

This brings us to the central question of the Christian religion, "Was Jesus Christ really God?" The answer to this question is called the Doctrine of the Incarnation.

Let us see first how it came about that a living man, Jesus of Nazareth, began to be thought of as God.

I ask you to recall for a moment the unusual history of the Jewish people. For two thousand years before Jesus lived they had believed in God as the personal creator of the world. To them the earth was the stage on which the drama of God's purpose was worked out. They were His chosen people.

Oddly enough, for the chosen people of God those two thousand years had been anything but a bed of roses. Once they had been enslaved in Egypt. For five hundred years they had to protect their homes and lives against attack from predatory neighbors. For three hundred years a disastrous civil war had raged between two factions of their own nation. At the end of this they were so weakened that they were easily conquered by the Babylonians, and the whole nation was taken into a new slavery that lasted nearly a century. When finally in the year 524 B.C. a remnant of them was allowed to return to Palestine to rebuild the nation's life, they were conquered and ruled over in quick succession by the Greeks (under Alexander the Great), the Ptolemaic kings, and by Rome.

This is the thing to remember: only once, for a very short time, did the Jewish people enjoy a golden age of peace, prosperity, prestige, and power. That was the age of the great King David and his son, King Solomon. It lasted from 1000 to 900 B.C.

Now, I ask you to think what your hope and expectation might well have been had you been a Jew at the end of those two thousand dreadful years of suffering. Would it not have been natural for you and all of your countrymen to long for the day when a great king like David might be raised up again to deliver you and your nation from subjugation and restore the golden age?

Of course it would! And this is why every pious Jew looked for the coming of a Messiah!

Notice, however, that the expected Messiah was to be pre-eminently an earthly king, as David was. All that the word Messiah meant to the average Jew was "The Anointed King."

Moreover, when he came, there were certain obvious specifications that he had to fulfil. No one who did not meet these requirements could claim to be the Messiah. What were they?

FIRST, *he must be born in Bethlehem.* The reason for this was simple. David had built Bethlehem as his crown city. Anyone born in Bethlehem was, therefore, considered a descendant of David. As a descendant, he was a lawful heir to the throne of Israel. Jesus was born in Bethlehem.

SECOND, *he must look like a king.* The Gospels speak eloquently about the electrifying effect Jesus had upon crowds wherever He went. Apparently, His bearing and size caught their imagination. Even John the Baptist picked Him out of a great throng and proclaimed Him Messiah. Evidently, Christ stood head and shoulders over the tallest of men.

THIRD, *he must speak words of wisdom and authority.* This we know was true of Jesus. The common people were thrilled. They said, "He does not speak like the Scribes and the Pharisees, but as one having authority."

FOURTH, *he must be able to relieve the suffering of his people.* Jesus did not do it often, but He did heal people. And this greatly enhanced His reputation.

FINALLY, *he must be a great warrior.* The real responsibility of the Messiah was to raise an army, drive out the hated foreign conqueror, and restore the glorious, prosperous reign of his remarkable ancestor David. This Jesus consistently refused to do, and this is why Judas Iscariot betrayed Him. It was because the Romans were afraid He might attempt to do this that He was killed upon the Cross.

Into this world, longing for deliverance, came Jesus of Nazareth. He possessed every one of the qualities that gave a Jew the right to claim that he was the Messiah, and there is no doubt in the Gospel record that He thought of Himself as the long-expected Saviour. Everything He did and said sprang from the conviction of His Messiahship.

Now, notice how He interpreted what the Messiah should accomplish. The Jews waited for a divinely sent human being to bring forth earthly prosperity. They called this "restoring the Kingdom of God."

To Jesus the Kingdom had an entirely different meaning. To Him it was essentially the rule of righteous love in the lives of men.

The Jews expected the Messiah to raise an army and defeat Rome. This Jesus rejected. Instead, He called upon the Jews to repent their sin and renounce every other ambition save that of becoming personal examples of loving sacrifice for their fellowmen.

A source of bewilderment to His own disciples, a living irritation to official Jewish religious leaders, increasingly feared by the local Roman authorities, He accepted the full implication of His unswerving devotion to righteous love. This led Him to His own death upon the Cross.

It is no play on words to say that now we have come to the crux of the whole astonishing life of Jesus of Nazareth. If the Cross had finished Jesus, it would have finished His disciples too. When He died, their hope for Him as the expected Messiah also died. When He was buried, they scattered in despair.

But Christ did not stay dead! He rose from the dead! It was the Resurrection that revived and confirmed their faith that they had not been mistaken in Him.

But still their understanding of their Risen Lord

was very incomplete. They had no immediate insight into the nature of the work to be done, nor any initiative to set about doing it.

He appeared to them five times and on the fifth occasion bade them wait until the Holy Spirit should come to empower them. They waited. Then came the Day of Pentecost. It was then that the great change came. From that day on, they and their successors have carried His name as God to the ends of the earth.

This is how a Jew, who lived two thousand years ago, came to be identified as God in human flesh.

So far none of this has been difficult for us to understand. Up to this point, we have dealt only with facts of history. These facts presented the world with something unique in human experience. Now we no longer have an ordinary man to deal with. We have a risen man, and a risen man whose influence on other men has been so great that they only have been able to describe Him by saying, "Somehow He is God."

How can anyone be both man and God?

The Christian Church always had the greatest difficulty explaining how this was true.

For six centuries, it struggled to put it into simple words.

Finally, the best statement of the Doctrine of the

Incarnation that the Church has ever had was set down in the Athanasian Creed.

Listen carefully to what it says:

> For the right Faith is, that we believe and confess: that our Lord Jesus Christ, the Son of God, is God and Man;
> God, of the Substance of the Father, begotten before the worlds: and Man, of the Substance of his Mother, born in the world;
> Perfect God, and Perfect Man: of a reasonable soul and human flesh subsisting;
> Equal to the Father, as touching his Godhead: and inferior to the Father, as touching his Manhood.
> Who although he be God and Man: yet he is not two, but one Christ;
> One, not by conversion of the Godhead into flesh: but by taking of the Manhood into God;
> One altogether, not by confusion of Substance: but by unity of Person.
> For as the reasonable soul and flesh is one man: so God and Man is one Christ.*

This is the orthodox Christian belief about Christ. It cannot satisfactorily be explained, but any other way of thinking about our Lord does not fully account for the historical events recorded in the Bible, nor for the continuing experiences of men ever since.

Let us then come back from early days to the present time.

* From The Book of Common Prayer of the Church of England.

Why is this doctrine important to you and to me today?

The answer is not hard. It has always been easier for some to appreciate Jesus Christ in two ways that are totally different from the genuine Christian understanding of who He is.

On one hand, it is easier to see Him only as a man. Admit that He spoke as no other ever spoke; that He taught as no other ever taught; that He lived as no other ever lived. As such, He is our dearly beloved example of what a good man ought to be. He is not, however, to be worshipped as our God.

If this be true, then God has not dealt with man's evil and man's sin. You and I can be inspired, but we cannot be forgiven. You and I can strive, but in the end we shall be defeated. You and I can hope in life beyond the grave, but our hope may, indeed, be vain.

This humanistic view is not only contrary to the historical evidence of the New Testament, it is not religion. It is merely ethical culture.

On the other hand, it is almost as easy for some to see Christ as only divine. These find it hard to accept the genuine human life of Jesus. They who believe this are religious but are likely to be sentimentalists or seekers after escape from pain and suffering. To these, God did not suffer on the Cross. If He did not cope with the physical and mental hardship of human life, then God has done nothing real that can bridge the gulf between Him and me.

It is only when we tenaciously hold to the conviction that our Saviour was both God and man that we avoid losing our grip on a God Who is able to save and help us.

It is because we believe that God was in Christ, reconciling the world unto Himself, that the Gospel is Good News to a sinful and suffering world.

WHAT ABOUT THE TRINITY?

WHAT ABOUT THE TRINITY?

. . . that which we believe of thy glory, O Father, the same we believe of the Son, and of the Holy Ghost, without any difference of inequality.—PRAYER BOOK, p. 79

I HAVE pointed out earlier in this series, first, that our Faith begins not by speculating about what God is like. It begins by looking at history to see what He has done. God is known to us by His mighty acts. Therefore, the belief upon which all other Christian doctrine rests is a belief in Revelation.

Then I asked that you think about God's creation. We saw that there are only three ways to interpret the universe that He has made.

We can describe it as a meaningless accident. But if it is a meaningless accident, life can have no greater purpose than to get all you can for yourself and "to hell with anybody else." Our sense of decency tells us, however, that this crude and cynical materialism can not be true.

We tested the opposite idea, the idea that the pantheist holds. To him the universe is completely filled by God in every part, so that

> All nature is but art, unknown to thee,
> All chance direction, which thou canst not see:
> All discord, harmony not understood;
> All partial evil, universal good.

This is definitely more attractive, but its trouble is that it is too attractive. Its weakness lies in what it overlooks. Everything in life is not that rosy. Such an explanation of the universe may have been all right for beautifully upholstered eighteenth century ladies in lavender and old lace. But pantheism is hard to swallow in a world where the memory of Hitler and Stalin does not make for pretty dreams.

So we concluded that in the universe two things are real: the God Who created it, and the evil that spoiled it.

We then had to wrestle with the problem, "If God is good, what is He doing about evil?" The Christian believes that God became a Man and had a showdown with evil upon the Cross. Jesus of Nazareth broke the back of evil by dealing it the sledge hammer blows of an absorbing love so powerful that evil could not destroy the integrity of His life. This is called the doctrine of the Atonement, and by this example of love we are to live.

In the fourth of this series we faced the question, "Was this man, Jesus of Nazareth, really God?" If God solved the problem of evil by living and dying as a man, how could such a thing be? The belief that God took upon Himself our flesh and blood is the doctrine of the Incarnation.

Now we are ready to tackle the hardest question in the Christian Faith. "If God became a man, what does this do to the idea that there is only one God?" How can God be the Father in Heaven, the Son Jesus Christ, and the Holy Ghost? The answer to this question is the doctrine of the Trinity.

As we start to think about the Trinity, I hope none of you will fall into the attitude that is common to a good many Christians. I fear many are of the opinion that the doctrine is either too difficult to understand or that it is not important to daily life. In regard to the first assumption, there is some truth. A Trinitarian God is not as cozy an idea as a Unitarian God. In regard to the second assumption, however, if anyone holds it, it but reflects a bad Christian education. The Trinity is so important to Christian living that, if you do not grasp its significance, you will never be able to adequately live the religion it describes.

Let us begin by getting a clear picture of the Trinitarian belief. I will put it into my own words first and then I will give you the official statement of the Church, in the words of the Athanasian Creed.

It is the Christian belief that there is only one God. But in this God there are three distinct Persons. They are God the Father, Who made us, God the Son, Jesus Christ, Who saved us from the effect of evil and Who is present with us in Holy Communion, and God the Holy Ghost, Who guides us and gives us spiritual strength.

This is the simplest way I can put what we believe into a few sentences.

Every church member, however, ought to recognize the more explicit official statement. Here is what the Athanasian Creed says:

> . . . the Catholick Faith is this: That we worship one God in Trinity, and Trinity in Unity;
> Neither confounding the Persons: nor dividing the Substance.
> For there is one Person of the Father, another of the Son: and another of the Holy Ghost.
> But the Godhead of the Father, of the Son, and of the Holy Ghost, is all one: the Glory equal, the Majesty co-eternal.
> Such as the Father is, such is the Son: and such is the Holy Ghost. . . .
> The Father is made of none: neither created, nor begotten.

> The Son is of the Father alone: not made, nor created, but begotten.
> The Holy Ghost is of the Father and of the Son: neither made, nor created, nor begotten, but proceeding. . . .
> And in this Trinity none is afore, or after the other: none is greater, or less than another;
> But the whole three Persons are co-eternal together: and co-equal.

I think you will agree that this should leave no doubt in anybody's mind as to what exactly the Christian belief is: There is one God. In God are three Persons. No one of the Persons is greater than the other. I think you will also say, "What a terrific test of the human imagination it is to try to picture such a situation!" But do not give up. Let us see now why the Church came to hold such a concept of God.

I am going to state why without any trimmings whatever. The unadorned fact of the matter is that the earliest Christians had a new set of experiences of God which could not be explained in any other way.

Many people think that Christianity began with the simple words of Jesus and that later mischievous, hairsplitting theologians made up complicated doctrines for some strange reason.

Actually, Christianity began with a very complicated religious experience; and in order to explain it simply, the first Christians had to break open some long-cherished, old-fashioned religious ideas because these old ideas no longer conformed to what experience taught them was true.

That men should find it necessary to do some revolutionary thinking certainly should not surprise us today!

Columbus broke up the old idea that the earth was flat when he sailed the Atlantic Ocean.

Louis Pasteur broke up the old idea about the origin of diseases when he developed the germ theory.

Einstein smashed the Euclidean universe to pieces with his new theory of the structure of the universe and, in doing so, made possible the smashing of the atom.

In like manner the early Christians, out of the necessity of what they had experienced first-hand about God, had to smash up the limitations men thought were inherent in monotheism. Their experience of the Trinity showed that while monotheism was true, it was even more remarkable than men had realized.

I have said that Christian experience forced the development of the idea of the Trinity. You are probably saying, "What does he mean by Christian experience? If he can make that clear, then I can see the whole idea!"

In *The Faith of the Church* there is an excellent

description. Picture to yourself a young Roman citizen who knew a few Christian friends. One of the things that struck him about them was that in some strange way they were remarkably changed. When he asked questions, they were more than eager to tell him about their new life. As a result he decided to attend one of the meetings of the group to which they belonged. While he did not understand much of what went on—worship, they called it—it certainly was apparent that this group was dominated by an *esprit de corps* such as he had never before known.

This powerful Spirit was doing remarkable things with these people. It gave them the courage to face torture. It made them share their possessions. There was a kindness and thoughtfulness about them he had not believed possible anywhere.

Thus, without knowing it, our Roman friend was beginning to have an experience of God, the Holy Spirit.

As he found himself attracted time and again to the meetings of this Spirit-filled group, he began to learn about One called Jesus. He found that these people were what they were because of their faith in Jesus. The time arrived when that which Jesus had said and done became so important to him that he found his whole set of values and his conduct changed. Christ had in fact become the Lord of his life.

Nor was this Christ a faraway name and example. In time he learned to feel His unseen Presence when the group worshipped and communed. This was an experience of God the Son.

As he learned more about Jesus, he also learned about the Father Who had sent His Son and Who had created all things. For the first time in his life the abstract faraway idea of God became personal, real, and powerful. By now he had an experience of God the Father.

Do you not now see what had happened to this young Roman? He had experienced God in three different ways. Each experience was valid and each was very real. He had a Trinitarian religion before he had a Trinitarian theology to describe his experience.

This young Roman was not alone. This threefold experience was the common experience of the early Church. It was the experience of the Twelve Apostles (and it has always been the experience of Christians in every age). Thus, it was inevitable that the Church had to revise the old-fashioned Unitarian idea of God.

The disciples and the Church experienced a new and wonderful life with Christ. He was so unique that they could not describe Him except by saying, "This man was and is God."

They lived and shared this remarkable new life by

the power of the Holy Spirit, which had first appeared at Pentecost.

This is what I meant when I said that Christian experience forced the development of the idea of the Trinity.

The upshot of all this was that the old-fashioned, limited, Jewish idea of monotheism was revised to include the new Trinitarian experience. Monotheism was not abandoned. It was retained but now it was seen to be more mysterious, more wonderful, than ever before.

Most people today begin their thinking about God with a conviction about His unity. If they do, then the Trinity, as an idea, is a complicated mystery.

I suggest that this is both historically and religiously wrong. Start, as the disciples of Christ started, with a clear understanding of your own experience. First, you are part of the Spirit-filled Church; then you come to know the Christ Whom the Church holds before men; and finally, through Christ, you have the love and the forgiveness of the Father Who made you. When this is the way you start and because this experience is so clear-cut and understandable, it will not be the Trinity that will be mysterious to you, but it will be God's unity that you will reverence as a great and wonderful mystery.

If you do this, you will easily understand the Collect for Trinity Sunday that says, "[We] acknowledge the glory of the eternal Trinity, and in the power of the Divine Majesty to worship the Unity . . ."

WHAT ABOUT THE CHURCH?

WHAT ABOUT THE CHURCH?

. . . and upon this rock I will build my church;—MATT. 16:18

THERE is one thing about the beliefs of the Christian that must have impressed you. Have you noticed the logical consistency that runs all through them? One doctrine leads in a common sense fashion to the next.

Our religion is not an insult to the intelligence. Because it does make clear sense, it produces a high degree of religious certainty. This certainty strengthens our personal faith and is the secret of God's power to help us. And this is why theology is so important. When you really understand the Christian Gospel, then what God has done to help you begins to bring results.

We come now to the last doctrine we shall consider in this series. This is the doctrine of the Church.

Let me place before you one of the most interesting and most controversial scenes in the New Testament (Matt. 16:13-18):

> When Jesus came into the coasts of Caesarea Philippi, he asked his disciples, saying, Whom do men say that I the Son of Man am?
> And they said, Some say that thou art John the Baptist; some, Elias; and others, Jeremias, or one of the prophets.
> He saith unto them, But whom say ye that I am?
> And Simon Peter answered and said, Thou art the Christ, the Son of the living God.
> And Jesus answered and said unto him, Blessed art thou, Simon Bar-jona: for flesh and blood hath not revealed it unto thee, but my Father which is in heaven.
> And I say also unto thee, That thou art Peter, and upon this rock I will build my church; and the gates of hell shall not prevail against it.

Let me dispose of the controversy first. You all know that the Roman Catholic Church uses this text to bolster its arrogant and silly claim that it alone is the true church. It does so by interpreting it to mean something like this:

Christ said to Peter, "upon you, a good solid rock of a fellow, I will build my church." Since Peter is alleged to have been the first bishop of Rome, and since the diocese of Rome is the primatial diocese in the Roman Catholic Church, it is therefore unconvincingly argued that our Lord gave Peter a place of supremacy above the other disciples. And the Church which Peter founded becomes, according to this view, the one and only true Christian Church.

This is historical nonsense, of course, but that is not the worst part of it. The worst part is that it is grammatical nonsense as well.

When our Lord said "upon this rock I will build my church," the rock He was referring to was not Peter. He was referring to what Peter had just said about Who He was. When Christ said "I will build my church upon this rock," he meant that He would build it upon the affirmation "Thou art the Christ, the Son of the living God." In short the Church was to be built on the fact of the Incarnation.

It is not controversy, however, that we are interested in. We want, instead, to understand the doctrine of the Church.

Like everything else in the Christian religion, the Church is the common sense result of practical necessity. We have seen that God has acted in history to do something to help man fight a winning battle against evil. We have seen that the most important thing that God has done was to have become a Man. We have seen that in Jesus Christ a new quality of human life was made possible for us who have faith in Him. We have seen that the early Christians, who knew Jesus, actually possessed a life-changing spiritual power that made them new kind of men.

The practical common sense problem, therefore, was: How can this wonderful new life be made available to everybody everywhere? Obviously, if what God had given Man in Christ was to last and to have the power to change life on a global scale, some way of passing it on to others had to be found.

I ask you to think for a moment how many different ways were open to God to accomplish this. Actually you can conceive of only two.

God might have passed on the new creation, that was Christ, by some kind of physical inheritance. It certainly is within His power to change our genes and chromosomes if He wants to. But think what that would mean! If he had done so, we would have begun to be automatically good. We would have become automatons!

No, God had to find a way to make available to us the wonderful newness of life that was in Christ without tampering with our freedom. Consequently, what God did in Christ could not be passed on by physical inheritance. That left but one other way open to Him to accomplish His purpose. What was that way?

Think for a moment how people are molded and

changed inwardly and spiritually! Think of all that you have read about psychology. What is the most powerful life-changing influence in the world? Is it not the influence of group life? We become the persons we are because we have been gradually molded by group living since the time we were born.

A baby has little to start with but his physical inheritance. Put him in a good family and he will begin to become a good child. Put him in a bad family and he will soon show the evil effects of his bad relationships.

Almost every part of our personality, except the physical body we are born with, we receive from living in various groups. Our characters are the product of our group experiences. Our educations are acquired from group life. Our skills and talents are developed under group influences. We are, for the most part, what being in a group makes out of us. And the way we can be changed for the better or for the worse is directly related to a different group-influence changing our lives.

If this is so, was it not the most natural thing in the world for God to make a new kind of group to give to each one of us what Christ had brought into human life? This is precisely what God did do. He created the Church to be a new kind of powerful group life. It is only within the Church's new and different fellowship that we can become the kind of man God wants each one of us to be. This is why the Church is necessary to God, and this is also the reason the Church is necessary for us.

Every once in awhile someone will say that he admires Christ, but that he does not see the need for the Church. The answer to that is obvious. Unless Christ had organized a group in which His new quality of life could be found, no one could ever have been a Christian. Without the Church, what God has done about evil, could not be passed on to benefit you and me. This is what is meant by the claim that life within the Church is necessary to salvation.

One thing needs to be underlined right here. If this life is to bring salvation, it must be in terms of realistic group living. Salvation means being changed into a new man in Christ. We are changed only by the power of group influence. Therefore, nominal participation in Church membership and occasional attendance at worship are incapable of changing anyone. Both make a travesty of what the Church is supposed to do to men. Both are dreadful sins because they reveal man's arrogance in taking the very instrument God has created and using it to defeat His holy purpose. If you have been casual about the Church, I plead with you to realize the enormity of what you are doing to Almighty God.

Up to this point I have tried to make two things

clear. First, I have shown how God makes available to all men what He brought into the world in Christ. Second, I have shown why this Church is necessary to God and to us.

There remains one question yet to be answered. How does the Church bring about the needed change in a human life? How do we become new men in Christ through the fellowship we share in the Church?

The gradual change takes place as the result of three actions we share together.

The first one is easy for us to understand. We are changed by what we learn in the Church. If you were born into a Christian family, you began to get a Christian education from the moment your mother took you in her arms for the first time. Long before you could understand any words, your father and your mother spoke the language of relationships to you. The love they showed toward you, the care they took of you, taught you the meaning of love before you knew the word to describe it. In time they taught you the difference between right and wrong. They taught you how to say your prayers. They taught you about God and Jesus. They brought you early to the Church to be baptized.

When you were old enough you went to Sunday school and there you learned many things, but especially how to worship God. At an appropriate age you were confirmed and began to make your Communion. At every great event in your life the Church has been there to teach you its deeper meaning. When you were married; when your own child was born; when you or your loved ones were ill; when someone in your family died; the Church ministered to you. The Church brought you the special gift of God's strength to help you. You heard sermons. You attended classes. You learned what God had done for you and all mankind.

Thus, the first way the group life of the Church changed you was to give you a Christian education. The first task of the Church is to teach men God's redemption.

But there is a second and more mysterious way you have been influenced. Probably you never knew that it was happening. But it always happens in every group you have ever been in, and the more active you are the more effectively it happens. Just living intensely amidst the invisible relationships with other people in the fellowship of the Church has had its effect upon you. Unconsciously you become like the group as a whole. You begin to think its thoughts. You acquire loyalty to its loyalties. You want to react as the group reacts. This unseen Spirit is so strong that it does more to change you than anything you learn with your minds. It is here that the power of the Holy Ghost is strongly at work within the Church for your salvation.

But there is yet an even more powerful influence of the Holy Ghost in the Church. The place where the new quality of life in Christ is most strongly at work in us is in the corporate worship of the Church. Here our thoughts are centered on God. Here we meet the spiritual Presence of God in Christ face to face in Holy Communion. Here we are in complete relationship with God the Father through the Son and by the power of the Holy Ghost. Here we learn to practice the Presence of God. Here we feel the common life of the fellowship most intensely. Here we pledge our common loyalty to God's Holy Will. Here we offer our sacrifice of praise and thanksgiving, joining it with the sacrifice Christ made upon the Cross. Here we are in relationship with God and with the whole fellowship of the Church, past and present, in the Communion of the Saints.

And because all that the Church is and all that the Church can do for men happens most sharply when the fellowship is at worship, it is said, truly, that the real task of the Church in the world is to worship God. Without worship no man can have the newness of life that came to earth in Christ. Without worship man is powerless to overcome his sin. Without worship there can be no victory for us over evil. Without worship the world cannot be saved. Only when you worship can you become a changed and different and empowered new man in Christ.

How shall we conclude this series of sermons about the Christian Faith? You have watched the drama of God's mighty acts for our salvation unfold.

History offers every man two figures, each with a cup raised high in his hand. One of these figures is the poet Omar Khayyám. He represents the mad and futile end to which all men have come who have relied upon themselves, alone, to find the secret of the mystery of life. He says to you:

> Drink and drown your sorrows. There is no answer to the mystery of life.
> Drink for you know not whence you come, nor whither you will go.
> Drink and wring from the passing moment what pleasure may be caught, knowing the while that it is futility.
> Drink and forget for soon there will be no more of thee and me.

You can choose that answer if you will, and many of our neighbors do; yet forget not that there stands hard by a second figure. It is that of the Crucified and Ascended Lord. He, too, holds high another cup. It is the cup offered to you at the altar rail. It is the cup of His blood poured out in loving sacrifice. It is the cup of God's pursuing, unconquerable love. It is the cup of the hope of salvation for the world. And He Who was slain for man's sin holds high this cup, saying:

> Drink for this cup is red, like the love of our Father in Heaven.
> Drink for the Father has acted mightily in your behalf.
> Drink for I know whence you came and whither you will go.
> Drink for in my Father's house there are many mansions.
> Drink for evil can have no dominion over you.
> Drink and be of good cheer. I have overcome the world.

WHAT WE BELIEVE

ABOUT ETERNAL LIFE

WHAT WE BELIEVE

ABOUT ETERNAL LIFE

We are compassed about with so great a cloud of witnesses, that we, rejoicing in their fellowship, may run with patience the race that is set before us, and, together with them, may receive the crown of glory that fadeth not away.

PRAYER BOOK, P. 79

ALL SAINTS' DAY is the Feast of the Aristocracy of Christian history. All Souls' Day is the Feast of the Democracy of Christian history. Both of them remind us of the shortness and uncertainty of human life. Both of them raise the question, "What happens after death?"

This question has haunted the human mind in all ages. Where do we go? Is there a future life? What can it possibly be like? Every man wistfully wishes he knew. In all of human history only four possible answers have been given. These are extinction, transmigration, absorption, and probation which leads to damnation or salvation.

Some people believe in our extinction. Death is the end to them. Nothing else follows.

Others believe that the soul transmigrates up or down into another body living on this earth, and that we may become a reptile or a prince. Our behavior in this life destines our body in the next.

Some have believed that we are absorbed—sponged up as it were—into one great prevailing spirit. Individual identity is lost.

Many have believed that we are on probation here. They contend that life is followed by a further period of trial and that final perfect life comes to those who deserve it.

The first three of these beliefs are non-Christian. The last is the Christian Faith.

For none of these ideas is there any direct proof. However, lest anyone jump to a speedy conclusion that life after death does not exist, let him ponder the following:

First of all, what does Christianity believe about life after death? What the average Christian probably believes is not what Christianity teaches. The average man's view of heaven is naive. Many good church people think of life after death as a change from man to angel. Pearly gates, harps, and a set of feathery wings, along with a comfortable, clean, white cloud to sit upon are actually what many think Christian immortality means. What a ghastly existence, with nothing to do but twang celestially upon a harp and to be doomed to listen to other befeathered twangers throughout eternity! This is a childish idea of eternal life!

What, then, does Christianity really believe about life after death? It believes that you, just as you are at the time of death, enter a new way of life. You do not become an angel nor anything else. You, no better and no worse than when you died, continue. What for? To have eternal rest? That is for your tired, worn-out, earthly body. But you are not your body! To have the perfect reward at once? How silly! You are not good enough. To be judged, damned, and perhaps destroyed? How unfair without a further chance.

No! Life after death, to the Christian, is none of these things. Life after death, we believe, is a continued life of spiritual striving wherein greater holiness and character may be won. It is a further opportunity to continue what we have started here. It is a chance to grow in knowledge, not by a sudden gift of omniscience, but by further picking one's way through the problems of existence. It is a chance to have sturdier moral fibers but only after labors and temptations that further tax and test us. It is a chance to widen our sympathies and affections, not by the obtaining of the perfect life, but by increasing the opportunity to love more widely. In the life after death that Christianity teaches, there will be struggle, there will be work, there will be sacrifices to be made. This is the Christian belief. We shall live. We shall grow. We shall strive until we have accomplished something; until we have been made good enough by our striving to be fit to live in perfect companionship with God.

This is a manly and noble conception of the next life. It should never cause us fear. Death is the grand adventure. What comes is no pale world of flitting spirits. It is a glorious place with opportunity to stride gallantly ahead. Nor should we be sorry that our beloved die. Death to the Christian is the most beautiful transition in the mystery of life.

Now, what does the unbeliever have to offer against this Christian faith? There are people who find it hard to believe in life after death. I have much sympathy for them. I mean for the man who, having thought deeply about it, finds it hard to believe in eternal life. I have no sympathy for that cocksure type of man who, having disposed of the whole question by stating dogmatically that when you're dead you're dead and that's all there is to it, snaps his mind shut and never thinks about the question again.

I am thinking of the wiser objections to belief in life eternal. What are they?

Some people have felt that belief in a future life

is egotism. They tell us that we are merely attempting to cling to our own petty personal existence because it seems so important to us. George Bernard Shaw was such a person. "How awful," he wrote to a London paper, "to have me going on eternally battering out thousands of plays and millions of articles." He said that he felt the time would surely come, if such were the case, when he would want to get down on his knees before God and ask if there were not some way of bringing such an insufferable process to an end. He maintained that only an egotist of the worst variety would want his existence to continue.

That argument seems high-minded! But did you ever sit at the bedside of someone whom you loved and watch him die? You may never have been able to believe in immortality for yourself, but it will be impossible for you ever to admit that the life of one whom you loved should be finished by death. This is proof that our belief in life after death is not egotistical, as some persons feel.

Another argument raised against the Christian belief is that it is an impulse to have a happy ending to every human story. There is, of course, a real shallowness among some men that makes them want a happy ending to their life. But the truth of the matter is that actually Man cares little or nothing about happy endings. You go to the movies and you are certain long before the plot is finally disclosed that you know the ending. You groan inwardly in boredom and disgust. The really great tale does not necessarily have a happy ending. Nor do we require it. Did *Hamlet* have a happy ending? All of its characters lay dead upon the stage. Yet *Hamlet* is the greatest drama in the English language. We care not one whit for a happy ending. Man really demands something far more satisfying. It is not the happy end but the worthy end he wants.

The great argument for a life which is not defeated in death is that otherwise the glorious work of God comes only to a shabby and indecent end. If death ends all, then the universe is a criminal blunder. We do not ask for a happy end for Man but we ask an end for him that is worthy of a righteous God.

The arguments against a life after death are less convincing to me than the arguments for it.

What, then, are the reasons for believing in a life after death? What indications do we have that such belief is not utter folly?

The difficulty we have in believing that there is a life after death is the difficulty of seeing how we can survive from one state to another. Is that not the great obstacle? Death seems so final. All that we recognize of a beloved one in death seems ended. No understanding lights the eye of the dead. The body becomes cold. Movement is at an end. Death does look indisputably final.

Yet, nature is filled with transitions as final as death appears to be. Wonderful to behold, life does survive. Let me give you an example:

A grub worm is swimming in a pond. He comes upon a frog and this might be the conversation between them. "Respected frog, you have been in two worlds, in the water and on land. Tell me what is there beyond my world of water?"

"Well," said the frog, as he puffed himself up with pompous importance, "the other world is just dry land."

"And what is that?" said the grub worm, "Can you swim on dry land?"

"Of course not," said the frog, "there is no water there."

"How can a world exist," asked the poor grub worm, "in which there is no water? What is there in this dry land?"

"It is all surrounded by air," said the frog.

"Air?" said the astonished grub worm, "What is air?"

The frog thought and thought and finally said, "It is the nearest thing to nothing that I know."

The poor little grub worm could not understand

dry land, and so he steadfastly refused to believe what the frog had told him.

One day a remarkable thing began to happen. The grub worm felt an irresistible urge to climb a lily stem. He found himself lying exhausted in the sun. He thought he was going to die. His skin dried. His joints cracked. His body shrivelled. And just when he thought that the end had come, he split open, and lo! he had become a dragon fly with wings of gorgeous hue.

There is an unbelievable survival in nature. Such a thing makes it easier for me to have faith in our eternal life. Or take another illustration of the great transition which all of us have experienced. Imagine, in that period when you were not yet born, what it would have been like had you had the power of thought. In those months you were living without light or air, cramped in a tiny space. What would you have thought? Surely you would have said, "This is existence! This is life! Beyond this state there is nothing more." Then suddenly came the violent transition of your birth. Before you lay a whole new world made more wonderful because you had lost your incapacity to understand.

God never creates in us capacities for which there is no use. Why are there ears and eyes in the unborn babe, if his dark silence is not to be followed by light and sound? Do you not see what this means? Man is equipped with his mind, with his intuitions, and with his love for something greater than this life. If this life be all, why have we been endowed with strange spiritual aspirations? If we can love now and cannot love eternally, if we can understand the universe in part and never understand it fully, if we can suffer so much, only in the end to be destroyed, then nature and God are irrational and cruel. Without eternal life our existence is unintelligible. With life after death everything in our crazy-quilt existence begins to make some sense.

The great proof of life after death is Jesus Christ. Listen to Him: "Because I live ye shall live also," and "Let not your heart be troubled, ye believe in God, believe also in me. In my Father's house are many mansions: if it were not so, I would have told you. I go and prepare a place for you . . . that where I am, there ye may be also. . . . Let not your heart be troubled, neither let it be afraid." Think of what those words assert. There are no ifs and ands, there is no "I think" nor "I hope" nor "I believe" in His statement about life after death. He says, in simple matter-of-fact fashion, "If it were not so I would have told you."

Did He speak the truth? We know that He came nearer the truth about life than any other man. Jesus

Christ is startlingly accurate when He speaks about human behavior. So astonishingly right is He about life that He remains today the great teacher for the majority of men. Is it not logical to believe that a man thus wise, a man so thoroughly acquainted with the secrets of life, so thoroughly informed upon everything that affects human destiny, knows what He is talking about when He speaks on the ultimate destiny of mankind? The Risen Christ and His statement that "in my Father's house are many mansions" are the unshakable grounds of my belief in eternal life.

What shall we say then of this feast of All Saints and All Souls? This is its message.* Have no fear of death for death has no harm. Beyond its doors stretches a lovely world of eternal opportunity. Rejoice therefore in eternal life. We "are compassed about with so great a cloud of witnesses, that we, rejoicing in their fellowship, may run with patience the race that is set before us, and, together with them, may receive the crown of glory that fadeth not away."

* I am indebted to the Rt. Rev. George Craig Stewart, at one time Bishop of Chicago, for some of the basic material in this sermon.

WHAT THE

RESURRECTION PROVES

WHAT THE RESURRECTION PROVES

And while they yet believed not for joy . . . he said unto them, Have ye any meat? . . . and he did eat before them.—LUKE 24:41, 43

SOME OF YOU will remember a novel, written half a century ago, by Ernest Poole. It was called *The Harbor*. One of the characters reminds us of many of our neighbors today. He was convinced that the past had nothing it could teach us. "History," said he, "is just news from a graveyard."

I suppose it never occurred to him, but unwittingly he gave a remarkable description of Easter Day.

Easter is "news from a graveyard"! And what glorious news it is! Someone has described it this way: "Easter is not an argument. It is an announcement. It is not a syllogism. It is a shout!"

Whatever else Easter may be, it is a triumphant proclamation of good news. And this news comes from where news of any kind is least likely to come

—from the symbol of the final defeat and humiliation of Man's most noble hopes. The good news of our salvation comes from a graveyard.

Let us see what this good news from a graveyard has to say to us. What does the Resurrection prove?

It proves, first, that Jesus Christ was God. Think for a moment about the shock the Resurrection must have been to the disciples! As Jewish patriots, they had long carried in their heads a clear picture of what the Messiah was to be like. He was to be a great King. He was to be an attractive giant, a man's man. He was to be able to speak words such as no man had ever spoken. He might even be able to do rather astonishing things, such as heal the sick, because He was highly favored of God. He was to be a warrior like His idolized ancestor, King David. And someday, He was to sit on the throne of Israel and rule all the nations of the world. All this was the Messiah! Nevertheless, He was still to be only a man.

This is what Peter, James, and John, and every one of the disciples believed about Jesus. Suddenly, on Good Friday, He was killed by the civil and religious governments. And now, on the first day of the week, He was alive and in their midst again.

Not one of the disciples could, at first, believe it. When finally they did believe, they still could not understand how such a thing was possible.

But there was one thing each one of them did understand. It was that Jesus, the Christ, was certainly no mere man. It humiliated them to admit it to themselves because they were steeped in the Unitarian idea of Jewish monotheism, but their own five senses forced them to it. They had to say that Jesus of Nazareth was nothing less than God in human flesh.

It was the Resurrection that established the divinity of Christ.

Think for a moment what this means to us. From the beginning of history mankind has been aware of the existence of God. The universe speaks of Him in a thousand different ways. The very life of man itself constantly throws off broad hints that, behind it—guiding, caring, strengthening—there is an unseen Power that can only be called divine. "Yet no man," as Holy Scripture says, "has seen God at any time."

Then to our utter amazement, God, whom the finite mind of human beings can only dimly apprehend, appears (out of His love for us) in the form of a man. At last, we can see God in terms that we are able to understand. In Jesus Christ, all that God is is brought into focus. We no longer need to wonder about God. We do not have to build our faith on speculation about what He is like. What God really is stands clearly revealed in the Resurrected Christ.

It is no wonder that we sing and shout on Easter

Day, "Alleluia! The Lord is risen! He is risen, indeed, Alleluia!"

The Resurrection proves something more. It proves that the power of goodness is actually stronger than the power of evil. Strange, is it not, that it took a graveyard to teach us this?

Nearly all of our experience of life seems to lead to the opposite conclusion. How often we are hurt by those whom we love the most. How frequently the dishonest person appears to flourish and to prosper. How obvious it is that scheming, selfish, hard-hearted people elbow their way to the front and get away with it. How silly it appears not to believe that God is not on the side of wealth, influence, and the worldly favored. How dare we think that might does not make right. How natural for all of us to echo the psalmist's words:

> I was grieved at the wicked: I do also see the ungodly in such prosperity. For they are in no peril of death; but are lusty and strong. They come in no misfortune like other folk; neither are they plagued like other men. . . .
>
> Lo, these are the ungodly, these prosper in the world, and these have riches in possession:
>
> And I said, Then have I cleansed my heart in vain, and washed my hands in innocency. . . .
>
> Then thought I to understand this; but it was too hard for me . . .—PSALM 73

Well, you and I have to admit, don't we, that that is the way life often looks? Evil appears to be greater than goodness. And what is more, it appears to be far more rewarding.

But wait a moment! This is not the end of the story. God's universe is not really like that at all! There is such a thing as the inevitability of the moral law. In the long run, righteousness is greater than evil. The wicked receive the just reward of their wrongdoing. Goodness cannot be ultimately defeated.

How do we know? We know because we have seen it demonstrated by Jesus Christ. The more evil struck Him down, the more He refused to let it destroy the integrity of His goodness. The more He suffered, the more He loved. And He loved most as He was dying!

Suppose now, such a one as this had remained dead? Suppose the graveyard answered only to such unyielding love with the silence of eternity? Suppose there had been no rising from the dead? Could we poor humans say anything except, "Then thought I to understand this; but it was too hard for me"?

If there is anything at all to goodness, it cannot be allowed to come to such a shabby and unworthy end. The ringing message of Easter is that it did not. For God raised up His Son on the third day. And the King of Love stands triumphant over pain, over evil, and even over death!

What happened in the Resurrection confirmed the words with which the psalmist had ended his lament:

> Until I went into the sanctuary of God: then understood I the end of these men;
> Namely, how thou dost set them in slippery places, and castest them down, and destroyest them. O how suddenly do they consume, perish, and come to a fearful end!—PSALM 73:18, 19

What the psalmist had learned in the sanctuary, was now proclaimed to the whole world from a graveyard.

Easter rings out its reassurance to all disappointed, despairing, doubting, burdened people everywhere. Be of good cheer, the tyrants, the sleazy shysters, the crooks and gangsters, the dishonest politicians, the easy-money people, the gougers, the selfish ruthless egotists, the power-mad crazy men, the self-appointed saviours of themselves (at the expense of everybody else), the whole kit and boodle of the wicked and unrighteous are wrong, and they do not really count.

What does count is what Jesus was like. The things that endure are "love, joy, peace, long-suffering, gentleness, goodness, faith, meekness, temperance: against such there is no law." (Gal. 5:22-23.)

It is this power of goodness to come through in victory that makes the message of Easter the best of all good news.

There is yet another strange thing that the Resurrection proves. Jesus rose from the dead, not as a spirit, but with a remarkable new body. This indicates that it is your ultimate destiny and mine to have a resurrected body similar to the new body of our Lord. That is why, at the end of the Apostles' Creed, we say: "I believe in the Resurrection of the body."

The Christian Church has always made this an important article of Faith, but it has been extremely careful not to attempt to put its stamp of approval on any speculation as to the nature of the body we shall have.

Saint Paul wrote the finest words in Holy Scripture on the subject when he spoke to the Church at Corinth:

> But some men will say, How are the dead raised up? and with what body do they come? . . .
> God giveth it a body as it hath pleased Him. . . .
>
> All flesh is not the same flesh: but there is one kind of flesh of men, another flesh of beasts, another of fishes, and another of birds.
>
> There are also celestial bodies, and terrestrial: but the glory of the celestial is one, and the glory of the terrestrial is another. . . .
>
> So also is the resurrection of the dead. It is sown in corruption; it is raised in incorruption:
>
> It is sown in dishonor; it is raised in glory: it is sown in weakness, it is raised in power: It is sown a natural body; it is raised a spiritual body. . . .

> as we have borne the image of the earthly, we shall also bear the image of the heavenly . . .
>
> thanks be to God, which giveth us the victory through our Lord Jesus Christ.—I COR. 15:35-57

So Easter Day reminds us of a good thing. Our bodies are a gift to us from a loving Creator. They are not to be pampered! But neither are they to be abused. They are the temples of our soul!

It behooves each one of us to treat our bodies with respect. We shall have them with us throughout eternity. The Risen Christ, Who offered the nail prints in His hands to the touch of doubting Thomas, Who entered the room where the disciples were ("the door being locked for fear of the Jews"), Who asked the disciples if they had any meat, and did eat before their eyes—this same Jesus is our reassurance that we shall recognize our loved ones after death in their bodies that we knew here. His Resurrection assures us that our whole being is so precious to God, our Maker, that not one part of it is deemed worthless in His loving eyes.

For all that Easter proves, we thank Almighty God:

> On Easter Day our praise we sing
> To thee, our risen Lord.
> Our love and life to thee we bring,
> O thou eternal Word!
>
> We turn from toil and weary loads
> And find our rest in thee.

We drink beside life's dusty roads,
  Thou fount of Galilee!

We raise to thee, this Easter Day
  Our praise of joyful song;
For unto thee, the truth, the way,
  All joy and praise belong.*

*John W. Shackford, "An Easter Hymn," *The Pulpit,* March, 1953, p. 17. Used by permission of The Christian Century Foundation.

DO YOU WANT

INWARD POWER?

DO YOU WANT INWARD POWER?

GRACE is inward Power! When you find nothing too difficult, when you live without fears, when you possess calmness amidst troubles, when you are confident within, when you can live without the ravages of tension, then you are in a state of Grace.

Grace is the religious name for the mysterious, elusive, personal secret of inner peace which nine out of ten men are searching for in this modern day. If you read Joshua Liebman's *Peace of Mind*, you were looking for Grace. If you watch Bishop Sheen on television, Grace is what you hope to get from what he says.

People hunger and thirst after Grace though they know it not by its religious name. They want, almost with a savage desperation, that which feeds the emptiness and inadequacy of their inner lives.

There are many ways of finding Grace. Some men find natural Grace in the warmth and love of human companionship. Some find it in the soul-feeding power of a great art like music or painting. Many find it in the creative activity of hobbies or a career. These are all healthy, beneficial ways to acquire Grace. But there are also evil and alluring substitutes that give promise of at least temporary release from the pain of soul in many men, for when men drink excessively, when they drown themselves in pleasures, when they seek solace or blankness in narcotics, it is still Grace they seek, and it is Grace they desperately need.

So universal is the human striving after Grace, and so much of human energy is poured forth day and night to get it, that it is no wonder this is what the Bible and religion are all about.

Consider, then, *the conditions under which real Grace*—healthy Grace, God-given Grace, religious Grace, life-saving Grace—*comes to you.*

For make no mistake about it, Grace is not to be had merely for the wishing. If it were, there would be no distracted, no nervous, no harried people in the world. If it were, the madness of living which you see all around you in the big city would cease to be. No—that inner peace of soul, which all men seek so passionately, comes—of this we can be sure—but it comes only in certain well-known and well-tested ways, and always at a price. It is because the price of spiritual peace is high that most men try first to get it at bargain rates. There are plenty of spurious substitutes that look cheap and satisfactory on the surface, but not one of them can bring real peace of soul. There is only *one* way; and in the long run it also, as you would expect, costs the least. For what is more costly than to spend a whole life madly searching for that which satisfies, and come to the end of the search bitter, disillusioned, and in despair?

Let us see, then, what are the conditions we must meet if we are to acquire peace and inward power, which is this thing called Grace.

We can picture these conditions graphically, I believe, by using an incident out of the pages of the New Testament.

Jesus had been talking to a group of people about their deepest inward needs. He concluded his remarks by taking a child up into His arms and saying, in effect, "Look at this little child. Here is an example of what peace of soul is! If you want what all of you are searching for, then you must become as this little child." Here is a perfect picture of what it means to be in a state of Grace. This, I take it, is what Jesus meant when he said, "Verily I say unto you, Whosoever shall not receive the Kingdom of God as a little child shall in no wise enter therein."

Now note what happened. "And a certain ruler asked him, saying, 'Good Master, what shall I do to inherit eternal life?' " (I point out in passing that the phrases "Kingdom of God" and "Eternal Life" both mean exactly what we are talking about—that wonderful enduring quality of inward power called *Grace.*) And Jesus said unto him, "Thou knowest the commandments, Do not commit adultery, Do not kill, Do not steal, Do not bear false witness, Honor thy father and thy mother."

And he said, "All these have I kept from my youth up." Now when Jesus heard these things, He said unto him, "Yet lackest thou one thing: sell all that thou hast . . . and come, follow me." And when he heard this, he turned away sorrowing.

What does this teach us about the conditions under which Grace comes? Notice first that a soul-satisfying Grace of God has nothing whatever to do with how well off we are. This is no down-and-outer, at the end of his rope, who thus appeals to Jesus. He was a rich young ruler! He had been born to a position of enviable privilege. He was a man of consequence in the world. He had power and authority. Moreover, he was no worn out, world-weary, aging cynic. He was young, healthy, and filled with a normal man's passion for life. And yet somehow all of this did not bring him inward peace, and he knew that there was something more that he did not have.

This means that a first condition of possessing Grace is the abandonment of any notion that peace of soul can be gained by expecting to find it through getting up in the world. In fact, it is a common experience that, by itself, success is more times than not a bitter disillusionment. Does this mean that we should have no ambition, or that we should not strive to accomplish something? Not at all! What it does mean is that we should have the good sense to know that *getting* is not synonymous with *living;* that *saving for a rainy day* is quite different from *being saved;* that *redemption* is not a *banking term;* and that *making a name and place* is no *guarantee that one will lay hold of that elusive spiritual treasure known as Grace.* St. Francis of Assisi didn't own the shirt on his back, but he was one of the happiest men who ever walked this earth. Jesus Christ did not have a home, nor an extra change of clothes, and when He died they gambled for the shirt on His back; but He had a Grace which has been unforgettable, and He strides across the history of mankind—a living rebuke to man's mad scramble to find peace in outward things.

When we finally realize that what all of us are most ardently seeking cannot be found in the place where most men look for it, in material outward things, then we have met and faced the first condition under which inward power really comes.

What else does the incident of the rich young ruler teach us? Consider, next, the meaning of Jesus' reply to this man's statement that he had kept all the commandments from his youth up! Think how you might have spoken had you been Jesus! Would you not have been tempted to compliment the man? "Good for you," you might have said, "you have been an unusual model of proper behavior. Surely Grace will come to you." But Jesus did not think that mere goodness was enough! I wish modern Christians would understand this! We will not find peace of soul just by striving to be good! How different was Jesus' insight! "One thing thou lackest . . . sell all that thou hast . . . and come, follow me!" What was the one thing lacking? Do you recall the little child which Christ had taken in His arms a moment earlier? What was the one stupendous quality of that little youngster's life? Was it not the quality of trustfulness? Here you have the second condition under which Grace comes. "Whosoever will not receive the kingdom of God as a little child"—trusting God and taking Him for granted—"shall in no wise enter therein." Our name for trust is Faith. *God's Grace comes only to a man who begins to have a personal trust in a badly needed Saviour.*

Is not this exactly what is wrong with the religion of so many people today? Think for a moment about your friends. Think for a moment about yourself. To most people religion means one of two things. It either means living a good life or it means accepting certain beliefs about God. The first is what religion meant to the rich young ruler. But Jesus said it was not enough. The second is what religion means to a college sophomore. It is not enough either.

Real religion is first, last, and always a personal relationship of trust in God.

There are only two truly unique experiences in life. One is falling in love and the other is getting real religion. Both of them have one thing in common—they are experiences of personal relationship.

Notice that both are ventures into the unknown. No one who has not experienced either can possibly understand what it is like, and he who has experienced both can never adequately describe what happened. But, if it is genuine, it makes all the difference in the world. Falling in love with the right girl always makes a new man, and a better man, and a happier man. And falling in love with God—for that is what a real personal trust in God amounts to—is the same as being born again into a new life of inward power, happiness, and peace.

There is one further condition under which Grace

comes. Jesus said to the rich young ruler, "come, follow me." The Grace of God pours abundantly into a *committed life.* The major reason why many people find so little real help from their religion is that they have never really committed themselves. Tepid commitment brings lukewarm rewards. The uncommitted life is the powerless life. Sideline religion is no religion at all. You cannot be neutral about Jesus Christ and still call Him Lord. Listen to Him speak, "He that findeth his life shall lose it; and he that loseth his life for my sake shall find it."

There was much wisdom in the old Athenian law of the reign of Pericles. The Greeks understood the destructive power of neutrality. They provided that "if an insurrection began—those who started it should be banished—those who stopped it should be rewarded—but those who only watched and did not take sides—these should be killed as enemies of the state."

Dante saw how fruitless was the uncommitted life when he described the scene in his *Inferno* where he beheld, suspended between heaven and hell, a group of people in utmost torment. "Who are these?" he cried, and his conductor answered, "Speak not of them—they are those who gave their lives to nothing—now heaven cannot receive them and hell will not have them!" What symbols they are of the futility of the uncommitted life. Not good enough for hell!

My message to you then is—if you want the inward power of Grace, give your life to Jesus Christ. Open your life to His invasion. Identify yourself actively with His cause. Take a definite stand daily with the Church which holds high His banner. Bend your back to the load of the work for a Christian man to do. A world is in travail. You are needed.

When you no longer seek for security in outward things; when you have at last a deep personal trust in God; when you have given your life to Jesus Christ; then and then alone will you have Grace—peace and inward power!

WHY YOU NEED CHRISTIAN GRACE

WHY YOU NEED CHRISTIAN GRACE

I thank my God . . . for the Grace . . . which is given you by Jesus Christ.—I COR. 1:4

THE SCOTTISH PEOPLE have produced great preachers. One of the greatest of these was a clergyman named Ian Maclaren. He preached compellingly on every conceivable Christian subject, but he always maintained that the most important Christian idea was found in the word Grace. He once said, "The very center of the Bible is the doctrine of the Grace of God."

Before we consider Why You Need Christian Grace, let us be sure that we all know *what the Grace of God is.*

Joseph Fort Newton, one of our great Anglican preachers, reported a conversation with a British soldier concerning a sermon he had heard. The subject was The Grace of God, and Tommy said, "The minister told us the Grace of God is plentiful, sufficient for all need. But sir, there was one thing he left out —he did not explain what the Grace of God is!"

Let us start with its meaning in ordinary speech. Suppose you were at Rockefeller Center watching the figure skaters. You probably would say, "How *graceful* are these skaters!" What you mean to express is, "How beautiful to watch is the movement of good skating." The word Grace means first of all beauty.

Now suppose that on the same day you meet a very charming person who seems particularly pleased to know you, and later you say, "Wasn't Mrs. So and So a *gracious* person!" The word Grace here means one who is concerned to make people happy.

In every day language, then, the word Grace can be summed up like this, *Grace is a beautiful concern that tries to make people glad.*

If we follow this jewel of a word into the pages of the Old Testament, it then, suddenly, takes on a sharp religious meaning. There, Grace is *the beautiful concern of God for sinful, unhappy men.*

Is that not a wonderful idea? But that is not yet all its meaning. Something far more wonderful is going to happen to its meaning as soon as Jesus Christ lights up this Word!

The great idea that dominates the New Testament

is that God not only had a concern for Man, but did something about His concern when He sent Christ to give saving strength to men!

So you clearly understand now the Christian meaning of Grace. *It is the life-changing spiritual power obtained from Jesus Christ.* St. Paul knew from personal experience what that inward power could do to a man, and that is why he wrote this text: "I thank my God . . . for the Grace . . . which is given you by Jesus Christ." He was thanking God for an inner strength that had made a new man out of him.

To put the whole Christian religion in a nutshell: *You too can have this inward power and it can make a new man out of you!* Notice, however, not just a "better man"—not just your old self spruced. No! The Grace of God will go one better. It will make a *new* man of you. *This is the Good News of the Gospel.* This is why Ian Maclaren said, "The very center of the Bible is the doctrine of the Grace of God."

Before we go further, I want to emphasize something I hinted at when I described how the word Grace had one meaning in the Old Testament, and a new and much bigger meaning in the New Testament. I pause to do this because many of my Christian friends are really Old Testament Jews and do not know it. What they understand to be Christianity isn't really Christianity at all. It is the religion of the

Old Testament, not the religion of the New Testament.

Remember, I said that, in the Old Testament, Grace meant "the beautiful concern of God for sinful man." Suppose you had been an Old Testament Jew living at the time when it was first realized that God cared —really cared—for a person like you, that He loved you so much that He yearned and yearned for you to be better and happier than you were. If God's love meant anything to you, your reaction certainly would have been, "If God is so concerned about me, I want to be a better person, because I care about Him too." You would have said to yourself, "I'll try—I'll *really* try to be good, because God loves me."

And that is exactly what every conscientious Old Testament Jew tried to do. He tried to be a good man. The whole Hebrew nation tried for a thousand years to be good. No group of people on earth have ever been so sincere about trying to be good.

And if you know your Bible you know what happened. For all their trying, they were not really good at all! Some of them finally simplified the whole business of being good into the keeping of a long list of superficial external rules. The most fanatic rule-keepers became known as Pharisees. The rest of the Jews knew that deep inside, where it really counts, they were not good; they knew that they were sinners. And yet, they wanted to be good for their own sakes as well as for the sake of God, who they knew loved them. Their own power to be good was not enough to save them. So they had happen to them what always happens to anybody who tries to be really good on his own ability—they were filled with frustration and despair.

The prophets had taught God's love, but knowledge of God's love by itself could not make them good. These great moral teachers had taught them what right conduct was. But knowledge of the Law was powerless to help them. They knew they needed something else. But they did not know what it was they needed!

Then came Jesus Christ—and those Jews who believed in Him suddenly discovered to their astonishment that their belief acted on them like a magic formula. They became new creatures. For the first time in their lives they were able to be really good. It was not a matter of just keeping rules. They possessed a new spirit and a new power. Something changed inside them. They described it as becoming "new men in Christ." This happened to hundreds—and has continued to happen ever since—and this life-changing power is what Christianity is all about. Also, this is what many Christians today know nothing about. To them Christianity is the call to lead a better life. I beg of you, do not confuse this with the real

Christianity! No man can lead a really good life by himself! No man can keep the moral law under his own power today any more than he could before Christ. If you try it, you almost certainly will become a modern Pharisee, satisfied with the outward appearance of respectability, or a frustrated neurotic. Both are legion all around us!

If you have been heroically striving to be a good Old Testament Jew, and wondering all the time why your religion lacked something, I plead with you to give the Grace of Jesus Christ a chance.

Shortly before his death, Dr. Charles P. Steinmetz, the great scientific genius of the General Electric, was interviewed by a well-known newspaperman. The reporter asked Steinmetz to state what he believed would be the most important scientific discoveries of the near future. He foretold the whole new realm of atomic discovery that has now come true, but he went on to say something further: "The greatest discoveries of the near future," said he, "will be in the realm of the inner spiritual life of man."

There are, within easy grasp of every man, invisible resources that are able to enrich our souls and make out of us new and happier men.

In the Epistle to the Ephesians, St. Paul calls these invisible resources of which Steinmetz spoke "the riches of Grace."

The astounding thing is that we need to be persuaded to take possession of these riches. A friend of mine describes it this way. Becoming a real Christian is like waking up suddenly and finding that you are a millionaire. All of us are spiritual millionaires. We have untold riches at our fingertips. "But the trouble," says he, "is that so few Christians know how to write checks on their spiritual wealth."

When you were baptized and confirmed, you became the owners of a vast spiritual estate. God, who loves you, wants you to take it, and use it, and enjoy it.

Do you remember the story of Raffles, the notorious jewel thief? It was his habit never to take all the booty? When he was finally caught and questioned about this curious habit, he replied, "Why, sirs, I have always been surprised at my own moderation!"

You do not have to purloin the riches of God. They are yours for the asking. And there are Christians who ought to be ashamed of their moderation.

THE MEANS OF GRACE

THE MEANS OF GRACE

Because strait is the gate, and narrow is the way, which leadeth unto life, and few there be that find it.—MATT. 7:14

IN THINKING of the Means of Grace, let us recall that Grace is the religious name for inward spiritual power. All men seek this constantly, even though they know it not by its religious name. The longing and the search for it is more universal than hunger and more compelling than sex. But it is never had merely for the asking, and there are not a thousand ways from which to choose to obtain it. Jesus knew this when He said, "strait is the gate, and narrow is the way, which leadeth unto life, and few there be that find it."

It should be obvious to anyone who looks about him that there is something wrong with Man. The most intelligent people of every age in human history have realized that there is a strange contradiction in human nature. Man has always yearned for the good life. Yet, at the very moment when he has wanted it the most, someone does some evil thing which destroys happiness and hurts others. In the wave of optimism which followed the First World War, it was popular to believe that Man acted this way merely because so many people were still uneducated. No longer does anyone seriously believe that ignorance is the cause of the world's perplexing troubles. Man is most erudite, and we see clearly that an educated devil can be even more destructive than an illiterate peasant. Our very cleverness promises to destroy us. We are bitterly aware that there is something basically wrong with human nature itself.

Our irreligious neighbors know this full well nowadays. That is why they are frequently in a bad state of mind about the future. The old-fashioned idealist is disillusioned. The hard-boiled realist is cynical.

Christianity never shared the hysterical optimism about Man that characterized the 1920's. Neither does it believe today that the world is filled with madmen who are totally depraved. What it believed then, what it believes now, and what it has consistently preached for two thousand years is something far wiser and more mature than the extremes of optimism or despair. The Church has always proclaimed that God created Man, innocent of evil and therefore a creature that was good; that Man fell from this original state of goodness by his own deliberate choice into evil; that the whole drama of history since that time has been the drama of God's mighty act to redeem him and give him the inward power to achieve once again a new state of goodness.

What does this religious explanation of Man mean? It means that God has always intended that we should have a good life here on earth. As far as we can make out, everything in God's creation gets along pretty well except mankind. If God wants us to enjoy life, how do we explain the anguish and misery of so much living? The answer is not hard to come by. Obviously, when God created Man, He created him differently from every other thing. The stars in the heavens obey physical laws. The animals on earth are the servants of compelling instincts which rule their lives.

But Man, somehow, is different. To him God gave what He did not give to any other part of His creation. To Man, God allowed a limited amount of freedom. Whether you believe that God created the world by a long slow process of evolution, or that God created all things in six days and rested on the seventh, makes no difference. It is perfectly clear that original Man used his God-given freedom to choose to do deliberately that which had evil results. This action was the Fall. From that moment on human nature was changed. From that moment Man's personal possession of inward spiritual power has never been sufficient for his needs. From that moment onward Man, who was created for perfect relationship with God, for perfect relationship with other men, and for perfect inner peace of soul, has lived in a state of broken relationships and inward frustration. This state of brokenness, religion calls sin; and because we are all born into it, and cannot avoid it if we will, we share in conditions of broken relationships reaching back through nearly all of human history. This is known as original sin.

What a dreadful state of affairs it would be if this were the end of the story! And yet this belief is precisely what being a modern realist amounts to. You have heard them speak! Human nature is evil; you cannot change human nature. Therefore, expect the worst until Man's stupid self-seeking eventually leads him to destroy the whole of mankind in some future holocaust.

To all the weary, disillusioned, and cynical, the Christian religion says, "Not so!" Man is evil, but this is not the end of the story! God, who created human life, does not intend to leave Man lost in his fallen evil nature. He has forever striven to restore the lost power for goodness which Man once had. This is the meaning of history. In every age and in every race of Man, there have been those enlightened and inspired men who have hungered and thirsted after righteousness and sought to find the secret of possessing that inward gift of spiritual power which all have recognized as needed for laying hold on righteousness. This is what primitive learning was reaching after. This is what philosophy has been all about. This is the essence of true religion.

The culmination of it all came when God, in His infinite mercy and compassion, intervened in human life Himself to save Man from his fallen nature. In the fullness of time God, who in the earlier times had spoken to Man through His prophets, became a Man and spoke to us through His only-begotten Son Jesus Christ, our Lord. He took fallen human nature upon Himself. And just as human nature had changed in the Fall for the worse, so it changed in the Incarnation of Jesus Christ for the better. Ever since Christ lived and died and rose again, a man who believed in Him could share in the restored nature of goodness. Faith in Christ brings the inward spiritual power which makes it possible to live righteously and possess inner peace. Unlike the change that took place when Man fell, the change that Christ brought cannot be inherited by physical birth. Each man by his own deliberate choice must come to have complete Faith in Christ first; then he will experience the miracle of spiritual rebirth. This is what Jesus explained to Nicodemus, "Marvel not that I said unto thee, ye must be born again."

So we come to the place where we can understand *what the Means of Grace are.* They are a series of actions instituted by Christ, or resting upon His teachings, which bring an extraordinary gift of inward power to those who have Faith at the ordinary moments of deepest human need. In the language of religion we call these means of Grace sacraments. The sacraments of the Church are normal ways by which normal men and women, who have come to believe in Jesus Christ, receive unusual amounts of inward spiritual power to feed and strengthen their Faith.

The first of these sacraments is Baptism. Christianity believes that in Baptism the contamination of original sin is done away with. By Baptism a man shares in the life and power of Christ. He is united with the Incarnation. His human nature is changed by God away from the tendency to do evil and set once more in the direction of doing good. But in spite of the fact that Man's fallen nature is changed in Baptism, he still cannot of his own power lead a good life. He constantly needs the further help of God. He constantly needs to be fed the strength of God. Baptism is the first condition of salvation. But it is only the beginning of the Christian life.

The baptized person learns that there are six other sacraments or means for obtaining the constant help of God. The first one open to him is Confirmation. He is ready for it when he is grown up enough to understand his need of God's help. In Confirmation his restored human nature is given a great gift. It is the gift of God's Holy Spirit. With it, he is newly strengthened and confirmed to do that which is right. In addition to the gift of the Holy Spirit, he is given the privilege of making his communions.

Holy Communion is the next great help of God constantly available to furnish the spiritual strength to live the good life. The baptized and confirmed Christian makes his communions regularly and frequently, receiving each time at the altar rail the Divine Body and Blood of the Incarnation, uniting his weak but restored nature to the strong and perfect Divine Nature. Holy Communion is the Christian's greatest and most frequent source of help. It will create great changes for good in any man who seeks it regularly and well. The weak, it will make strong; the tempted, it will give the power to resist; the confused, it will clarify; the discouraged, it will encourage. The defeated, it will make victorious.

But these are not all the sources of spiritual strength Christianity provides. For the heaviest responsibilities of life and for the greatest crises, there are special sacraments. The heaviest responsibility of life is entered into when one marries. Here an individual life ceases to be responsible to itself. It is responsible now for its goodness to its mate and to its children. Grave are the consequences to each member of the family and society as a whole if the heavy responsibilities of matrimony are not fulfilled. Man needs spiritual strength for this. This special strength comes in the Sacrament of Holy Matrimony.

The two great crises of life are sickness of the soul and sickness of the body. The symptoms of the sickness of the soul are frustration, discouragement, and fear, and a consciousness of sin. A consciousness of personal failure and sin always lies at the base of frustration, despair, and fear. To give new life where sin has destroyed peace of mind, God in Christianity provides the Sacrament of Penance and Absolution. Here, in full confession, a man's conscience is set right with God. He receives God's forgiveness and absolution and is inspired to make a clean start again. It is a great pity that in our Church the Sacrament of Penance is so little used. If any man be burdened with frustration, despair, fear, or a consciousness of sin, I urge him to make an appointment with his priest and receive the forgiveness of our loving God.

Sickness of the body is the other great human crisis.

To combat it man needs all his spiritual strength. God in the Church provides this help in the Sacrament of Unction. I have known people to be cured of infirmities by it. I have known many others to be spiritually comforted so that their bodily pain was healed or made bearable.

Nor did God in Christ leave this ministry of saving inward power difficult to find. In order that it be available to every man, He entrusted this ministry of reconciliation into the hands of special stewards, the apostles of His choosing, and gave to them a special sacrament of Grace to enable them to minister worthily to His children. This last sacrament is called the Sacrament of Holy Orders. We possess it in our Church in the threefold order of bishops, priests, and deacons.

If all this be true, how then would you define a Christian life? You have been told that a Christian is not one who merely believes in Christ and tries to live a better life. I think you can see from what I have said why this is true. No man, since the Fall, has had enough spiritual power of his own to be able to try to live a better life.

A Christian is one who realizes that, of himself, he is hopelessly lost in his struggle with life. Whether we like it or not, this is where true Christian living begins. From here, it proceeds to an understanding that what is needed is a Saviour in whom one can have implicit trust. The second step in Christian living is to say, "I really believe; God help mine unbelief." Then this feeble spark of Faith must be constantly fed in Holy Communion at all times, with the special means of Grace in times of crises. This is the pathway to salvation. There is no other way provided. Either we use it or power and peace will never come. "Because strait is the gate, and narrow is the way, which leadeth unto life, and few there be that find it."

MAKING LENT COUNT

FOR SPIRITUAL GROWTH

MAKING LENT COUNT FOR SPIRITUAL GROWTH

Sing, O barren, thou that didst not bear . . . Enlarge the place of thy tent . . . stretch forth the curtains of thine habitations: spare not, lengthen thy cords, and strengthen thy stakes. ISA. 54:1-2

No conscientious Churchman should hurry into Lent without giving thought. Shrove Tuesday is a poor day upon which to decide what your use of Lent will be. He who makes a few hasty Lenten resolutions on Ash Wednesday usually finds his high resolves dwindling before the following Sunday. Therefore, I call upon you to plan to make Lent count for your spiritual growth.

Nowhere in the Bible is the spirit and the purpose of Lent better described than in the famous Chapters 53 and 54 of the prophecy of Isaiah. Chapter 53 is prophetic of Good Friday and describes the Suffering Servant of God:

> He is despised and rejected of men; a man of sorrows and acquainted with grief . . . surely he hath borne

> our griefs, and carried our sorrows . . . he was wounded for our transgressions . . . the chastisement of our peace was upon him; and with his stripes we are healed . . . and he made his grave with the wicked, and with the rich in his death; because he had done no violence, neither was any deceit in his mouth . . . and he was numbered with the transgressors; and he bare the sin of many, and made intercession for the transgressors.

These words give us the purpose of Lent. The Christian Church observes Lent in order to remember and to share the humiliation and the suffering of God's Son, Jesus Christ.

But does this mean that the spirit of Lent is a doleful spirit? Indeed, it does not. The disciplines of Lent are not disciplines of desolation! Listen to what the prophet has next to say:

> Sing, O barren, thou that didst not bear; break forth into singing, and cry aloud . . . enlarge the place of thy tent, and let them stretch forth the curtains of thine habitations: spare not, lengthen thy cords, and strengthen thy stakes.

A Christian Lent can be summed up in this way: "It is kept because God's Son suffered and died. It reminds us of the painful cost of the Divine Love which saves us. Therefore, out of joyous gratitude we discipline ourselves that we may grow more Christ-like."

There is not a negative note in any part of a proper Christian Lent. It is the most positive season of the whole Church year. It is no call to descend into the valley of despair. It is a command to come up higher. It is a fast of forty days when we do joyous battle with the powers of evil and all the works of darkness.

The important words in the text of this sermon are all big, powerful verbs. They can be our cue to a Lent of spiritual growth.

The first word is *sing.*

"Sing, O barren, thou that didst not bear."

This indicates the spirit in which we are to keep Lent. I am not suggesting that you suddenly break into song on Ash Wednesday and literally go about your daily rounds warbling like a bird until Lent is over! Nor am I urging you to change overnight into one of those dreadful creatures who, suddenly gripped by the passion of renewed religious zeal, goes about dripping sweetness and light.

I *am* asking you, however, not to enter Lent with tightly drawn lips and a deathlike determination to see an unpleasant job through to the bitter end.

The proper spirit with which to keep a Holy Lent is to have in your heart the ordinary cheerfulness that always accompanies the prospect of a stimulating and worthwhile adventure. Lent is a special opportunity to become a better person. It is a short, intensive training period for the improvement of the body and the soul. It is a six-week therapeutic. It is a month and a half of jolly good fun wherein we engage in a real tussle with ourselves.

This is precisely what our Lord Jesus meant when He gave His famous rules for keeping a fast: "Moreover when ye fast, be not, as the hypocrites, of a sad countenance . . . But thou, when thou fastest, anoint thine head, and wash thy face; That thou appear not unto men to fast, but unto thy Father which is in secret."

Cheerfulness is the spirit with which to enter Lent. Sing, and give thanksgiving to God for the opportunity it brings us to remember God's love for us in Christ. Sing, and give praise to God by voluntary abstinence and self-discipline. Sing, and no longer be barren of the good works of the Lord.

The second cue word is *enlarge.*

"Enlarge the place of thy tent, and let them stretch forth the curtains of thine habitations."

The prophet is reminding the Jewish people of a scene that is familiar to every dweller in the desert country. He pictures for them the colorful oasis tent of the nomad. Because it had to be taken down and compactly folded for camel travel to the next water hole, the average tent never seemed to have quite enough room. I suppose times have not really changed. Just as the young couple in a small city apartment longs for just one additional room when its family begins to grow, so the Jewish desert wanderer always yearned to have a little larger tent. But a larger tent, like a larger apartment, is only likely to come to those who put forth the effort to earn one.

Now Isaiah was not really talking about tents. He was talking about the same thing that I am talking about.

All of us inhabit narrower and more cluttered mental halls than we need to dwell in.

"Enlarge the place of thy tent" is a valid Lenten call to each one of us to grow into a more spacious knowledge of our religion.

Just three years ago, a large group of Harvard freshmen were given an experimental religious literacy test. Every one was a Christian who had grown up in what passes today for a Christian home. Every one had been at one time enrolled in a Christian Sunday school. Never in the history of Harvard College has more misinformation appeared than in the answers to the examination questions. It was an almost unbelievable example of religious illiteracy when more than twenty-five percent of the students identified Jesus Christ as an Old Testament character! It was obvious, if this was typical of college freshmen all over America, that our youth could stand a considerable enlargement of the tents of their religious knowledge.

But, how about you? You are grown-up, sincere,

and obviously looking for real religion. How large is your habitation in your knowledge of your Church? Do you know the common facts about the Bible, our Church, our theological beliefs, our sacramental life? I hope you do! But I also hope you are not satisfied with what you know. I hope you will use Lent to "stretch forth the curtains of thine habitations."

The third cue word in our text is *lengthen.*

"Lengthen thy cords."

If you have been a summer camper you undoubtedly have been initiated into the mystery of the successful operation of a tent. You will recall that most tents are so made that cords of strong rope branch outward from the sloping roof to hold the top of the tent in place. These ropes are never knotted tight when they are secured. Instead, they are fitted with a moveable loop so that they can quickly be lengthened or shortened as need arises. *The length of a tent-cord depends upon the strain which weather puts upon the rope.*

Isaiah has used a striking illustration here. He calls to us to "lengthen thy cords." The ropes of a tent are always lengthened in stormy weather to ease the strain.

One of the most important uses of Lent is that it can be a time when we relieve the strain upon our daily lives. Nearly every one of us lives under a busy schedule of activities. We rush from one appointment to another, in frantic haste. Life in a city like New York is high-speed life. We subject our tortured nervous systems to a kind of punishment they were never intended to endure. We rush through day after day, fall wearily into bed at night, and wake up exhausted in the morning. The result is that, for many, there is no real joy in living. Excitement there is aplenty, but "the peace of God which passeth understanding" is an empty Prayer Book phrase. How few there are who know what it means to have the gladness of thanksgiving in their hearts, or who face each morning with the attitude, "This is the day which the Lord hath made; we will rejoice and be glad in it."

This futile fury of modern living need not be! It is taking years off the life-span of many people. It kills more of our neighbors than any other dangerous thing.

I, therefore, ask you to use Lent as a time to "throttle-down." For six weeks, reduce the breakneck speed at which you are going. This is one of the reasons why the Church wants you to "give up" things for Lent. No Lent is well-kept unless we obey the call of our Master Jesus Christ, when He said to His disciples: "Come ye yourselves apart into a desert place, and rest awhile."

You alone will know best what to take out of your daily schedule. Maybe it will be the bad habit of staying up too late at night. Maybe your social calendar needs to be radically reduced. Maybe you are serving on too many committees. People today are more nervous from trying to do good than from the dissipation of being naughty! Maybe you are a time-waster, who puts off until the last minute the things he ought to do with orderly leisure, and then madly drives himself into a frenzy to do them all at the last moment. If so, get some order into your life this Lent.

Whatever your besetting sin—which causes you to live tensely—whether it be pride or sloth, face it honestly, and get rid of it during Lent.

"Lengthen thy cords." Relax the strain!

The last cue word is *strengthen.*

"Strengthen thy stakes."

This is the call each one of us receives in Lent to drive deeper the shafts which secure our inner lives.

I am going to ask you to do only one thing in Lent that is exclusively religious:

I want you to take the time to pray!

I do this because, if you try to grow without praying, you will fail miserably.

Dr. Lewis L. Dunnington tells what prayer means to Roland Hayes, the great Negro concert singer. It is no easy matter to be born a Negro—even a gifted Negro—and Hayes had many humiliating incidents to bear as he traveled from one American city to another. He maintains that he never could have faced his burdens if he had not prayed constantly for help. When asked how he maintained his serenity, he said, "I try to live every moment with such a consciousness of the Divine Presence in my heart that every trace of bitterness shall disappear."

He never began a concert without standing silent before his audience to ask God's help in prayer.

One day his travel took him back to Alabama, and he went to visit the plantation where his mother had been a slave. The old master and his wife were still alive, but the years had reduced this once proud Southern family to poverty. Before them stood the son of a former slave. He had become famous and well-to-do. The words of the Magnificat were never more prophetic than at this moment: "He hath put down the mighty from their seat, and hath exalted the humble and meek. He hath filled the hungry with good things; and the rich he hath sent empty away."

Would you have blamed Roland Hayes if he had said, within a scornful heart, "How are the mighty fallen!"? But he did not do that. The lifelong praying he had done to overcome bitterness now saved him from the onslaught of pride.

He asked if there was anything he could do to help. He reached into his pocket and drew forth a check. It was the returns from several of his largest concerts.

He put it into the hands of the elderly mistress of his mother. When she realized the size of the gift, she burst into tears. In a moment, all three were in one another's arms—three of God's children, with no dividing line of color, bitterness, or hate.

"If a colored man," says Dr. Dunnington, "living in a white man's world, can live and work happily, triumphantly, and radiantly, so may you and I."

I agree with that, if you do what the colored man was wise enough to do.

"Strengthen Thy Stakes"—And pray!

HOW WE FAIL GOD

HOW WE FAIL GOD

And the Lord turned, and looked upon Peter. . . . And Peter went out, and wept bitterly.—LUKE 22:61

YOU DO NOT have to search any further than the Gospel for Wednesday before Easter to find the Bible's most striking description of the common ways in which we fail God.

We usually think of the story of the first Maundy night as being all about our Lord's institution of the Last Supper. It is that indeed. But it is also something else, something so terrifying that at first it is difficult to believe. Did you ever stop to think that on the night when Christ gave His Church the ever unfailing blessing of His continued Presence in Holy Communion, His own disciples failed Him most tragically in three different ways! What a contrast is Maundy Thursday! At the very moment when Christ demonstrates the love of God for men most faithfully—at that very moment His dearest friends betray Him.

As we watch their failure unfold before us, we should ask ourselves, "Have I, too, failed God in such a way and at such a time as this?"

The first failure of God took place that night in the Garden of Gethsemane:

> And he came out, and went, as he was wont, to the Mount of Olives; and his disciples also followed Him. And when he was at the place, he said unto them, Pray that ye enter not into temptation. And he was withdrawn from them about a stone's cast, and kneeled down, and prayed, saying, Father, if thou art willing, remove this cup from me: nevertheless not my will, but thine, be done. . . . And when he rose up from prayer, and was come to his disciples, he found them sleeping . . . And he saith . . . could ye not watch with me one hour?—LUKE 22:39-46

How did the disciples fail God in this scene? It is a common failure, and we have been guilty of it many times. *When Christ needed His friends the most, they failed to be reliable!*

Think what thoughts must have come into Jesus' mind as He looked down upon His sleeping followers! After three long weary years of careful training, after all that He had taught them, after they thoroughly understood from what had happened on Palm Sunday the danger He and they were in, after He had personally asked them to watch and be on guard, He found them sound asleep. They still were not dependable. They were untrustworthy.

I suppose there is no offense we can commit that will make men loathe us as quickly as the offense of being found unworthy of a trust. In the Army, a sentry who falls asleep on duty is given a summary court martial, and, if found guilty, is immediately shot. Why such swift and drastic punishment? Because his unreliability has exposed everyone to danger.

On the other hand, how deeply moved we are by any unusual example of dependability. Not long ago a picture appeared in the newspapers of a dog that refused to leave the spot on a river bank where his master had gone swimming and had drowned. The faithful dog had been set to guard his master's clothes. Though he did not understand why the familiar face did not return, he stayed for days and would not be taken away.

When an animal can be so faithful, it makes us, as persons, the more ashamed of our failures in dependability.

As we look at the sleeping disciples, we ought to ask ourselves if we have been reliable men and women. There is not one of us upon whom some other person does not depend. Someone looks to us for loving care. Do we always give it as we should? Someone looks to us for intimate companionship. Are we dependable? Someone looks to us as an example of how he should think and act. Have we lived up to the trust he has placed in us? Someone relies upon us to do some important part of the work of the world. How reliably do we carry out our responsibilities?

And what about our faithfulness to God? He depends on us as Christ depended upon Peter, James, and John. Are we dependable in worship? Are we reliable in work for His Church? Are we trustworthy in our giving?

In the Gospel of Saint Luke, Jesus asks a searching question: "when the Son of man cometh, shall he find faith in the earth?" Well, what kind of people are capable of faith? Only those who themselves are faithful. What will Christ find in your heart if He should come and ask an accounting of you? Will He find you reliable?

God was failed in a second fashion on the first Maundy Thursday night. This was the night that Judas Iscariot chose to betray His Lord. You recall the scene at the Last Supper:

> And as they sat and did eat, Jesus said, Verily I say unto you, One of you which eateth with me shall betray me. And they began to be sorrowful, and to say unto him one by one, Is it I? and another said, Is it I? And he answered and said unto them, It is one of the twelve that dippeth with me in the dish.—MARK 14:18-20

Thus Jesus foretold how He was to be betrayed by one of His very own. Now watch the fulfilment of his prophecy. It is one of the blackest moments in the history of mankind. We are in the Garden of Gethsemane:

> And immediately, while he yet spake, cometh Judas, one of the twelve, and with him a great multitude with swords and staves, from the chief priests and the scribes and the elders. And he that betrayed him had given them a token, saying, Whomsoever I shall kiss, that same is he; . . . And as soon as he was come, he goeth straightway to him, and saith, Master, master; and kissed him.
>
> —MARK 14:43-45

So ghastly and unbelievable is this scene that we want to turn our eyes away. It is terrible enough for anyone to betray a friend—but think of the duplicity that is laid bare here! Judas Iscariot betrayed Jesus by pointing him out to the mob with a kiss, the sign of intimate friendship and love.

How could he have done it? What was the motive for his betrayal? Was this failure merely the usual crass greed for gain that motivates so many men? No, I do not think so. Men are surely greedy, but even the greediest will hesitate to trade the life of someone whom they love for a paltry thirty pieces of silver. Surely, something more than the love of money lay behind this act!

The real motive behind this man's failure was impatience. Judas truly believed in Jesus, but he wanted Him to act as the Jewish Messiah was expected to act: to declare Himself King of Israel; to call the people to arms; to drive out the hated Romans; to restore the Kingdom to Israel; to rule the world.

When, after the momentous actions of Palm Sunday, at the very instant when it had seemed that Jesus was at last to rally the Jews to overthrow the power of Rome and suddenly He had slipped through the crowd and disappeared, Judas raged in disappointment. It was then that he threw all caution to the wind and decided to force the hand of Our Lord. He did not want to go on waiting any longer. He decided to point out Jesus to His enemies and put Him in a place where He would have to act like the Messiah of the Jews!

Judas thought that the thirty pieces of silver would buy the freedom of the Jewish nation. Instead, it bought the death of two lives, His master's and his own!

The impatience of a man nailed the Son of God to a cross.

Let us return to our self-examination. Do you ever fail God by your impatience? May I suggest to you that if you are a worrier, the real reason is that you are not a patient person! Did you ever think of that?

The most important lesson you have to learn if you are going to overcome worry is to practice how to wait. I will tell you something else. Do you know how to measure the extent of your trust in God? The measure of your trust is the same size as your capacity to have patience. The less you are willing to wait, the less you really believe in God.

Perhaps you do not worry much, but maybe you are the kind of person who cannot delegate responsibility to anyone else. Such men like to believe that they can do things much better and much faster than anyone they know. They pride themselves on their efficiency. Now capability is a wonderful thing. But do you know that behind the efficiency of some people, there really lies not self-confidence but fear? This fear makes them impatient. Unless they do everything, they are afraid nothing will be done quite right. Such people have no capacity for fellowship because they do not trust anybody. They cannot take the time to find out what others may be able to do.

Are you like that? Are you hiding a frightened soul under the protective cover of your impatience with other people? If you are, remember that Judas Iscariot was just like that. You should pray that with the help of God you will become more patient—more patient with other people, more patient with yourself, and above everything else more patient with God.

There is a third way to fail God. It, too, is revealed in the Gospel for Wednesday before Easter. Here is how it is related:

> Then they took [Christ], and led him, and brought him into the high priest's house. And Peter followed afar off. . . . But a certain maid beheld him as he sat by the fire, . . . and said, This man was also with him. And he denied . . . saying, Woman, I know him not. And after a little while another saw him, and said, Thou art also of them. And Peter said, Man, I am not. And about the space of one hour after another confidently affirmed, saying, Of a truth this fellow also was with him . . . And Peter said, Man, I know not what thou sayest. And immediately, while he yet spake, the cock crew. And the Lord turned, and looked upon Peter. . . . And Peter went out, and wept bitterly.
>
> —LUKE 22:54-62

What a climax of disappointment this must have been for Jesus! His disciples fell asleep when His life was in danger. He was betrayed by one of them with the sign of friendship. And now Peter, who had loudly protested at the Last Supper that he would follow the Master to prison and to death, denied that he was acquainted with Christ!

I sometimes think that the most terrifying scene in the whole Passion comes in the moment when "the Lord turned, and looked upon Peter."

In that look was concentrated all of God's bitter

realization of the failure of mankind. Here, for one fleeting instant in time, is revealed God's age-long frustration when faced with the sin of man. For once, God does not act or speak. He does not condemn nor does He encourage. All that He does is look. And in that look is focused all His sorrow, amazement, and compassion. If ever there was a moment when the pages of the Bible open up to us a window looking into the eternal heart of God, this is it. For a brief second all time stands still, as the Creator looks at what He has created. The only person who sees what is in those eyes is Peter. Is it any wonder that he "went out and wept bitterly"?

And yet we need to remember that it was not Peter that God was looking at! He was looking at mankind. He was looking at every man since Adam. He was looking at the sorry thing His creation had become as it reached feebly upward, groping for perfection, and slithered backward, down toward the earth's primeval slime from whence it had come. He was looking at the most promising and, also, the most irritating thing He had created. He was looking straight at you and me.

What do you suppose it was that redeemed us in the eyes of God? What made Him turn His look from Peter and determine that mankind must be saved?

Well, I'll tell you what it was. It was not what we

are, but what we can become! It was not what we have achieved but what we have in us yet to be. It was not as He saw us at that moment, but as He saw our human nature as it is in His beloved Son.

So Peter's failure is the culminating failure of the night when our Saviour was betrayed. But it is more than that. It is the symbol of the tragic failure of mankind since the Fall. In a real sense it can be epitomized by what happened to two men. In Adam sin began, and in Peter what sin did to Man stands pathetically revealed. When God looked upon both of them, their reaction was the same. They both wanted to get out of the sight of God and hide. "Adam and his wife hid themselves from the presence of the Lord God amongst the trees of the garden." (Gen. 3:8) "Peter went out, and wept bitterly." (Luke 22:62)

Whenever you and I fail God, we always want to hide.

Why does the Church re-enact each year every detail of the Holy Week story? It is to announce to you the Good News that you do not have to hide.

It is true that you have failed God. But God has seen something in you in which He still believes.

Come then out of the shadows of your sins. Draw near to the clear light of His redeeming love. Hide not your failures from His eyes. Confess, be forgiven, and be saved!

WHAT SAYEST THOU

OF THYSELF?

WHAT SAYEST THOU OF THYSELF?

Then said they unto him, Who art thou? . . .
What sayest thou of thyself?—JOHN 1:22

WHERE can one go to find a theme for a service to prepare us for the miracle of the Birth of Jesus Christ? It would be difficult to find a more perfect theme than that which is to be found in the Gospel for the Fourth Sunday in Advent.

Allow me to refresh your memory. John the Baptist was preaching in Bethabara, beyond Jordan. He proclaimed the immediate coming of the mighty Messiah. This greatly disturbed the Jews, and they sent priests and Levites to question him. So numerous had his followers become that many were saying that John himself was the Messiah. When the priests confronted him, they said:

> Who art thou? And he confessed, and denied not; but confessed, I am not the Christ. And they asked

> him, What then, Art thou Elias? And he saith, I am not. Art thou that prophet? And he answered, No. Then said they unto him, Who art thou? that we may give an answer to them that sent us. What sayest thou of thyself? He said, I am the voice of one crying in the wilderness, Make straight the way of the Lord . . . there standeth one among you, whom ye know not; he it is, who coming after me is preferred before me, whose shoe's latchet I am not worthy to unloose.

I want to point out three things which this incident reveals about John the Baptist. Try to think how these things apply to you.

John the Baptist was absolutely honest. When he was asked who he was, he immediately replied that he was not the Christ. Now, as strange as this may sound to you, John had every right to believe that perhaps he was the Christ. Every Jewish boy who could trace his family tree back to the great King David had that right. Whenever any male descendant of David accomplished anything to gain a reputation, everyone who knew him began to ask, "Can this be the long-expected Messiah?"

John was a famous personage. He was the famous preacher of his day. Moreover, he dressed and looked like the ancient hill country prophets of a bygone day. That is why, when he denied that he was the Christ, the priests asked him if he were the ancient prophet Elias come back to life. And he answered, "No!" What a temptation it must have been for John to hesitate and, without even saying a word, give the impression that—well, maybe; who can tell? There is a universally human tendency to delight in being associated with the great. How often we are tempted, when it is to our advantage, to bend the truth a little to fit our advantage.

Not so John! He left no doubt in anybody's mind. He answered a decisive no! He was absolutely honest. Had he not been honest, he would have stolen what belonged to the Son of God. Have you ever realized that when one is not honest, he is really a thief?

In the Old Testament Book of Malachi, there is a searching text. It asks, "Will a man rob God?" It is the rhetorical question with which the Old Testament ends, and in a way, sums up the whole spiritual searching of the first part of the Bible.

Well, go over to the end of the Gospels in the New Testament, and there you will get your answer. Look what men did to God on Calvary. They robbed Him of His liberty; they robbed the shirt off His back; they hanged Him high between two thieves and robbed Him of His life. Of course, men will rob God. They have been doing it persistently since the Fall. It is what unredeemed, fallen human nature, in its terrifying arrogance, always will do to God. Only a converted and committed man "will be honest to God."

Now, is there any standard by which we can measure our own honesty to God? You will find the best one in the Offices of Instruction in the Book of Common Prayer. The question is asked there, "What is your bounden duty as a member of the Church?"

The answer is given in five parts.

First, we are *to Follow Christ.* Well, have you? Remember, we are trying to be as absolutely honest as John the Baptist was: "What sayest thou of thyself?" To follow Christ means to put Him up ahead of you as your daily leader. Have you known Him well, or is He a distant, vague shadow in your life? Does He change your action and decisions in any way? Have you stopped in your daily choices to ask, "Would Jesus approve of what I am about to do?" Be honest! How much of an influence is Jesus Christ in your life? Maybe you have been very loyal to Him. God bless you if you have! But maybe you have not been much of a follower, after all. If so, be honest, and admit it now.

Second, we are *to Worship God Every Sunday in His Church.* Notice that we have been taught it is our bounden duty, as well as our blessed privilege, to worship God *every Sunday* in His Church. This is to be taken literally. Fifty-two Sundays a year, rain or shine; good weather or bad; summer or winter. There is only one bona fide reason for a Churchman's missing church on Sunday and that is illness.

"What sayest thou of thyself?" Have you been with Christ at the altar every Sunday? If you have, do not be proud! You are doing only the minimum required of you. If you have not been faithful, now is the time to say so and tell God you are sorry for your shameful neglect.

Third, we are *to work.* How much time have you given to the Church's work? Have you helped in a guild? Have you served as an usher? Have you worked with the choir or with the acolytes? Have you called on anybody to tell them about your church? There is a lot of hard work to be done for the spread of Christ's Kingdom. Every member of the Church owes God some work and some time. Have you been honest with God about your time?

Fourth, we are *to pray.* "More things are wrought by prayer than this world dreams of." Prayer is the real vocation of the Christian. Whom have you prayed for lately? Many friends of mine keep a little notebook for the names of those for whom they are praying. Do you say grace at meals in your house?

It is a poor Christian, indeed, who takes all that God has to give daily and never pauses to show that he is grateful. Do you pray for yourself? You need it most of all!

> Lord, what a change within us one short hour
> Spent in Thy presence will avail to make!
> What heavy burdens from our bosoms take!
> What parched grounds refresh us with a shower!
> We kneel, and all around us seems to lower;
> We rise and all the distant and the near,
> Stands forth in sunny outline, brave and clear;
> We kneel, how weak! We rise, how full of power!
> Why therefore, should we do ourselves this wrong,
> Or others—that we are not always strong—
> That we are sometimes overborne with care—
> That we should ever weak or heartless be,
> Anxious or troubled—when with us is prayer
> And joy and strength and courage are with Thee? *

Fifth, we are *to give.* How generous is your stewardship of money for the work of God? One of the things that makes me very happy is that most of the people who are members of Trinity Parish are not the rich people of New York. We are not the fashionable congregation of this city. We have many who are receiving middle-size incomes. We have many more who are living on very small incomes. And we have many who are very poor in worldly goods. But we are the largest parish in the City of New York. And I am not happy with the giving of many of our

* From *Prayer* by Richard C. Trench.

people. Each one of us owes a portion of his income to God. Let us not rob God! Let us give Him what is His!

"What sayest thou of thyself?" Are you doing your share? If not, I ask you to go to your clergyman and increase your pledge. If you have no pledge, go to him and make one! Now is the time to be a better steward of Jesus Christ. "What sayest thou of thyself?"

I ask you to consider a second characteristic of John the Baptist. You will note that he was a man who was not afraid to stand alone! He had the courage of his convictions. When he believed, he did not have to have the whole world believing the same thing in order to speak on behalf of his faith. When the priests and Levites asked him, "Who art thou?" he said, "I am the voice of one crying in the wilderness, Make straight the way of the Lord."

I admire anyone man enough to stand up for his beliefs. One of the great examples of this kind of courage is recorded in the Old Testament Book of Daniel. Three young Jewish boys, Shadrach, Meshach, and Abed-nego were brought before the Persian King, Nebuchadnezzar. He demanded that they fall down and worship a graven image. If they did not do so, they would be thrown into the midst of a fiery furnace.

Consider the courage of these three boys! What would you have done in their place? "What sayest thou of thyself?" This is how they answered the King:

> Our God whom we serve is able to deliver us from the burning fiery furnace . . . But if not, be it known unto thee, O King, that we will not serve thy gods, nor worship the golden image which thou hast set up.

How different that courage is from the abject, cringing confessions which the accused in famous Communist trials always seem to make today! My belief is that if one famous accused prisoner will stand up in court and defy his judges, the whole rotten framework of propaganda trials will collapse!

You and I are not put to the test as these Jewish youths were, nor as Communist prisoners are; but, we are daily put to the test!

How do you act when some friend or fellow worker ridicules our holy religion? Do you have the courage of your conviction to speak up with firmness for what you believe? How do you act when some smart aleck is blasphemous?

Our God needs those who will speak their minds on His behalf. Jesus Christ has no other voice but your voice to make this message heard. You may experience what it means to be a "voice crying in the wilderness"; but you will have greater self-respect if you stand courageously for your religion. Think of John the Baptist when you need courage. You never could picture him in silence when boldness was needed to speak for Christ.

There is a third quality which I admire in John. He was not only honest and courageous, he was also humble! Listen to what he thought about himself:

> There standeth one among you, whom ye know not; he it is, who coming after me is preferred before me, whose shoe's latchet I am not worthy to unloose.

As great a reputation as John had (and remember he was a national hero at this moment—his name was on everybody's lips), he still knew what his limited worth was. It takes real greatness to remain a humble man.

There is a story told about Toscanini, the greatest living conductor of our time. Once as he was rehearsing Beethoven's Ninth Symphony with the New York Philharmonic, he gave his musicians such a new feeling and insight into the music that, when the rehearsal ended, they rose and cheered him. Desperately, Toscanini tried to stop the ovation. When, finally, there was a lull, his shaken voice was heard exclaiming, "Toscanini is nothing! It isn't I; it's Beethoven!" He is a great man, as we all know, but much of his greatness lies in his humility.

Humility is the virtue that is truly Christian in its origin. Did you know that? Dr. Langmead Casserly has pointed out that a pagan thinks of goodness as a kind of higher self-assertion. It is the triumph of the will over fear and temptation. Christianity is not like that at all. Goodness, to a Christian, does not start with high self-assertion, but with an act of submission to God's will. Until Christianity came into the world, humility was regarded as a vice. A real Christian credits his sins to himself and his virtues to God's grace. The practical result is that in a true Christian integrity becomes unassumingly charming instead of coldly arrogant, as it did in the Jewish Pharisee. Without humility, goodness can be repulsive. The little girl understood this when she prayed: "O God, make the bad people good—and the good people nice!"

Dr. John Duncan was the greatest theological mind of Scotland in the first part of this century. Scholars came from all over the world to hear his brilliant lectures on mystic and ascetic theology. He was such a scholar and such a linguist the students claimed that when Duncan, who was affectionately known in Edinburgh as "Rabbi Duncan," said his bedtime prayers, he spoke to God in Hebrew. One day, two of them hid themselves in his bedroom to verify the rumor. This is what they heard:

> Gentle Jesus, meek and mild,
> Look upon a little child;
> Pity my simplicity;
> Suffer me to come to thee.

Dr. Duncan was not only great; he had the grace of Christian humility. Do you have any of it in your life? "What sayest thou of thyself?"

The Church never forgot who John the Baptist was. He was the man who prepared the way for the coming of the Lord Jesus Christ. What can the Church say of you?

In olden days, the King of Sparta was visited by an ambassador from another part of Greece. Said the visitor, "I am surprised to see that Sparta has no walls!"

"Come," said the King, "I will show you Sparta's walls." He led the ambassador out of doors and showed him ten thousand well-trained soldiers on the plain below. "There," said the King, "are the walls of Sparta. Ten thousand men, and everyone a brick."

The Kingdom of Christ has never erected walls. It has hurried down the centuries attempting to tear down walls. It has none of those things which the kingdoms of the earth prize to preserve themselves.

It has no cannon. It has no backlog of supply. It has no armament of any kind. But it does have one thing. It has converted men! That is all it needs. You are the walls of the Church of the Living God.

"What sayest thou of thyself?"

43–1053–HC–13